# Contents

**Funny Bunny Hat See p35**
**Little Folk Cardie p46**

Little Woodland Jacket p25

Foxy Hat p35

Little Owl Jersey p28

Little Cub Hat p35

# Little Woodland Folk

Little Owl Jersey p28

# Little Walking Jacket

Little Walking Jacket  p31

Little Owl Hat p35

*Cosy winter woolies for outdoor boys...*

# Little Owl Hoodie

Little Lumber Jacket p56
Foxy Hat p35

Little Owl Hat See p35

Foxy hat
little owl hat,
little lumber jacket

This little hat is an easy introduction to fairisle knitting – with buttons and simple embroidery for the eyes...

Little Owl Hat See p35

Little Snowflake
Blanket

Blanket p40
Tunic p43
Hat  p35

# Rosehip Tunic

# Little Folk Cardie

Funny Bunny Hat p35
Little Folk Cardie  p46

*simple textures,*
*little details,*
*easy to knit...*

**Willow Coat p48**
**Funny Bunny Hat See p35**

*Willow Coat*

A little star in his favourite hoodie

Little Star Hoodie p51

Pebble body warmer ....

Perfect for cosy winter layering

Pebble Body Warmer p54

# Sweet Little Heart ...

Little Petal Hat p35
Little Heart Jersey p51

*Little holiday blanket for cosy naps in the car.*

Little Petal Hat See p35
Blanket p40
Little Heart Jersey p51

Easy cables in cotton,
for those breezy days
on the beach...

Little Surfer Jacket p56

Summertime Blues... and greys

Little Holiday Jacket p59

Little Sailor Hoodie p54
Little Star Blanket  p40

*A splash of colour....*

Little Sailor Hoodie p54

Little Sailor Hoodie

Sunny Little Cardie p46

# Lazy Hazy days of Summer...

Little Garden Coat p25

Sunny Little Cardie p46

# Petal Pink...

Little Holiday Cardie p59

Pretty pastels,
easy textures & cables,
Adorable little knits ...

# Little Crocus Dress...

Buttons down the back for easy dressing...

# beach house babies

# Little Woodland Coat & Little Garden Coat

## MEASUREMENTS

### Ages

| Mths | 0-9 | 9-18 | 18-24 | 3-5 years | 5-7 years |
|---|---|---|---|---|---|
| **To Fit Chest** | | | | | |
| cm | 41-46 | 46-51 | 51-56 | 56-61 | 61-66 |
| in | 16-18 | 18-20 | 20-22 | 22-24 | 24-26 |
| **Actual Measurement** | | | | | |
| cm | 50 | 55 | 60 | 66 | 71 |
| in | 19¾ | 21¾ | 23¾ | 26 | 28 |
| **Full Length** | | | | | |
| cm | 28 | 32 | 38 | 42 | 48 |
| in | 11 | 12½ | 15 | 16½ | 19 |
| **Sleeve Length** | | | | | |
| cm | 17 | 20 | 24 | 29 | 33 |
| in | 6½ | 8 | 9½ | 11½ | 13 |

## MATERIALS

**Little Woodland Coat**  Baby Alpaca DK

| Shade 510 Cranberry | 50g balls | 3 | 4 | 5 | 7 | 8 |
|---|---|---|---|---|---|---|

**Little Garden Coat**  Cottonsoft DK

| Shade 710 White | 100g balls | 2 | 2 | 3 | 3 | 4 |
|---|---|---|---|---|---|---|

Also suitable for any King Cole DK yarns.
It is essential to work to the stated tension to achieve the correct size of garment.

### Needles
1 pair 4 mm (UK 8 – USA 6) knitting needles
1 pair 3¼ mm (UK 10 – USA 3) knitting needles
6 buttons

### Tension
22 sts and 28 rows to 10 cm, 4 in, over stocking stitch on 4 mm needles or the size required to give the correct tension.

## Little Woodland Coat

### BACK
Using 3¼ mm needles and thumb method cast on 66[70:78:86:94] sts.
**1st row.** * K2, p2, rep from * to last 2 sts, k2.
**2nd row.** P2, * k2, p2, rep from * to end.
These 2 rows are called **2x2 rib**. Work 3 rows more in 2x2 rib.
**6th row.** P7[7:8:7:5], p2tog, (p8[16:10:8:7], p2tog) 5[3:5:7:9] times, p7[7:8:7:6]. 60[66:72:78:84] sts.
Change to 4 mm needles and work as follows:-
**1st row.** K19[22:23:26:27], p22[22:26:26:30], k19[22:23:26:27].
**2nd row.** P19[22:23:26:27], k1, * (k1, p1, k1) all into next st, p3tog, rep from * to last 20[23:24:27:28] sts, k1, p19[22:23:26:27].
**3rd row.** As 1st row.
**4th row.** P19[22:23:26:27], k1, * p3tog, (k1, p1, k1) all into next st, rep from * to last 20[23:24:27:28] sts, k1, p19[22:23:26:27].
From 1st to 4th row forms **patt**. Cont in patt until back measures 15[18:23:26:31] cm, 6[7:9:10¼:12] in, ending with a ws row.

### Shape Raglan
Cast off 5 sts at beg of next 2 rows. 50[56:62:68:74] sts.
**For 2nd, 3rd, 4th and 5th sizes only**
Work [2:2:2:4] rows dec 1 st at each end of every row. [52:58:64:66] sts.
**For all sizes**
Work 24[24:26:30:30] rows dec 1 st at each end of next and every foll alt row. 26[28:32:34:36] sts.
Cast off rem 26[28:32:34:36] sts in patt.

### LEFT FRONT
Using 3¼ mm needles and thumb method cast on

42[42:50:54:58] sts.
Work 5 rows in 2x2 rib as given for Back.
**6th row.** P20[20:24:24:28], slip these sts onto a stitch holder, purl to end dec 2[0:2:3:2]sts evenly across row for 1st, 3rd, 4th and 5th sizes only and inc 1 st in centre of row for 2nd size only. 20[23:24:27:28] sts.
Change to 4 mm needles and work as follows:-
**1st row.** Knit.
**2nd row.** Purl.
Last 2 rows form **st-st** (stocking stitch).
Cont in st-st until left front measures 15[18:23:26:31] cm, 6[7:9:10¼:12] in, ending with a ws row.
### Shape Raglan
**Next row.** Cast off 5 sts, knit to end. 15[18:19:22:23] sts.
**Next row.** Purl.
**For 2nd, 3rd, 4th and 5th sizes only**
Work [2:2:2:4] rows dec 1 st at raglan edge in every row. [16:17:20:19] sts.
**For all sizes**
Work 14 [16:14:18:18] rows dec 1 st at raglan edge in next and every foll alt row. 8[8:10:11:10] sts.

## Shape Neck

Work 1[2:2:3:2] rows dec 1 st at raglan edge in next and foll 0[0:0:2nd:0] row **AT THE SAME TIME** dec 1 st at neck edge in every row. 6 [5:7:6:7] sts.

**For all sizes**

Work 8 [5:9:8:9] rows dec 1 st at raglan edge only in 2nd[1st:1st:2nd:1st] and every foll alt row. 2 sts.

**Next row.** P2tog. Fasten off.

## RIGHT FRONT

Using 3¼ mm needles and thumb method cast on 42[42:50:54:58] sts.

Work 5 rows in 2x2 rib as given for Back.

**6th row.** Purl to last 20[20:24:24:28] sts dec 2[0:2:3:2] sts evenly across row for 1st, 3rd, 4th and 5th sizes only and inc 1 st in centre of row for 2nd size only, turn and leave rem 20[20:24:24:28]sts on a stitch holder. 20[23:24:27:28] sts.

Change to 4 mm needles and cont in st-st until right front measures 15[18:23:26:31] cm, 6[7:9:10¼:12] in, ending with a rs row.

**Shape Raglan**

**Next row.** Cast off 5 sts, purl to end. 15[18:19:22:23] sts.

**For 2nd, 3rd, 4th and 5th sizes only**

Work [2:2:2:4] rows dec 1 st at raglan edge in every row. [16:17:20:19] sts.

**For all sizes**

Work 14 [16:14:18:18] rows dec 1 st at raglan edge in next and every foll alt row. 8[8:10:11:10] sts.

**Shape Neck**

Work 1[2:2:3:2] rows dec 1 st at neck edge in every row **AT THE SAME TIME** dec 1 st at raglan edge in next and foll 0[0:0:2nd:0] row. 6 [5:7:6:7] sts.

**For all sizes**

Work 8 [5:9:8:9] rows dec 1 st at raglan edge only in 2nd[1st:1st:2nd:1st] and every foll alt row. 2 sts.

**Next row.** P2tog. Fasten off.

## SLEEVES (Both alike)

Using 3¼ mm needles and thumb method cast on 34[38:38:42:46] sts.

Work 5 rows in 2x2 rib as given for Back.

**6th row.** P4, p2tog, (p10[5:5:6:4], p2tog) 2[4:4:4:6] times, p4. 31[33:33:37:39] sts.

Change to 4 mm needles and work in st-st inc 1 st at each end of 3rd and every foll 10th[6th:6th:8th:8th] row to 39[37:41:47:49] sts.

**For 2nd, 3rd, 4th and 5th sizes only**

Inc 1 st at each end of every foll [8th:8th:10th:10th] row to [45:49:53:57] sts.

**For all sizes**

Cont without shaping until sleeve measures 17[20:24:29:33] cm, 6½[8:9½:11½:13] in, ending with a ws row.

**Shape Raglan**

Cast off 5 sts at beg of next 2 rows. 29[35:39:43:47] sts.

Work 20[16:12:12:8] rows dec 1 st at each end of next and every foll 4th row. 19[27:33:37:43] sts.

Work 4[10:16:20:26] rows dec 1 st at each end of next and every foll alt row. 15[17:17:17:17] sts.

Cast off rem 15[17:17:17:17] sts.

## RIGHT FRONT BORDER

Using 4 mm needles cast on 1 st (cast on st to be used for sewing border to front), with ws facing, work across 20[20:24:24:28] sts left on a stitch holder for Right Front Border as follows:- p6[6:7:7:8], inc in next st, p6[6:8:8:10], inc in next st, p6[6:7:7:8]. 23[23:27:27:31] sts.

**1st row. (rs)** S1, purl to end.

**2nd row.** K2, * p3tog, (k1, p1, k1) all into next st, rep from * to last st, k1.

**3rd row.** S1, purl to end.

**4th row.** K2, * (k1, p1, k1) all into next st, p3tog, rep from * to last st, k1.

From 1st to 4th row forms **patt**. Cont in patt until right front border is of sufficient length to go up front edge to beg of neck shaping, ending with a ws row.

Cast off purlways.

Sew right front border in position using cast on st. (Buttonholes have not been made in the border as the buttons will push through the bramble st pattern)

**For a Boy**

Mark positions for 2 buttons level with each other 4.5 [5.5:6.5:7:7.5] cm, 1¾ [2¼:2½:2¾:3] in below cast off edge and 1.5 cm, ¾ in, in from each side edge of border.

## LEFT FRONT BORDER

Using 4 mm needles cast on 1 st (cast on st to be used for sewing border to front), with rs facing, work across 20[20:24:24:28] sts left on a stitch holder for Left Front Border as follows:- p6[6:7:7:8], inc in next st, p6[6:8:8:10], inc in next st, p6[6:7:7:8]. 23[23:27:27:31] sts.

**1st row. (ws)** S1, k1, * (k1, p1, k1) all into next st, p3tog, rep from * to last st, k1.

**2nd row.** Purl.

**3rd row.** S1, k1, * p3tog, (k1, p1, k1) all into next st, rep from * to last st, k1.

**4th row.** Purl.

From 1st to 4th row forms **patt**. Cont in patt until left front border measures same as Right Front Border, ending with a ws row.

Cast off purlways.

Sew left front border in position using cast on st. (Buttonholes have not been made in the border as the buttons will push through the bramble st pattern)

### For a Girl

Mark positions for 2 buttons level with each other 4.5 [5.5:6.5:7:7.5] cm, 1¾ [2¼:2½:2¾:3] in below cast off edge and 1.5 cm, ¾in, in from each side edge of border.

### BACK TAB

Using 3¼ mm needles and thumb method cast on 10[10:10:14:14] sts. Work in 2x2 rib as given for Back until tab measures 10[12:12:14:14] cm, 4[4¾:4¾:5½:5½] in, ending with a ws row. Cast off in rib.

### NECKBAND

** Join raglan seams. With rs facing, using 3¼ mm needles pick up and knit 20[20:24:24:28] sts evenly along top edge of right front border, 5[4:7:7:7] sts evenly along right side of neck, 11[13:13:13:13] sts from 15[17:17:17:17] sts cast off sts at top of right sleeve, 22[24:26:30:30] sts from 26[28:32:34:36] cast off sts at back of neck, 11[13:13:13:13] sts from 15[17:17:17:17] sts cast off sts at top of left sleeve, 5[4:7:7:7] sts evenly along left side of neck and 20[20:24:24:28] sts evenly along top edge of left front border. 94[98:114:118:126] sts. Beg with 2nd row of 2x2 rib as given for Back work 1 row.

### For a Girl

**Next row.** Rib 4, cast off 2 sts, rib 7[7:9:9:11], cast off 2 sts, rib to end.

**Next row.** Rib to last 12[12:14:14:16] sts, cast on 2 sts, rib 8[8:10:10:12], cast on 2 sts, rib 4.

### For a Boy

**Next row.** Rib to last 16[16:18:18:20] sts, cast off 2 sts, rib 7[7:9:9:11], cast off 2 sts, rib 3.

**Next row.** Rib 4, cast on 2 sts, rib 8[8:10:10:12], cast on 2 sts, rib to end.

### For a Girl or Boy

Work 2 rows more in 2x2 rib. **

### For a Girl

**Next row.** K4[6:6:8:4], k2tog, (k4, k2tog) 11[11:13:13:15] times, k4[6:6:8:4], cast off rem 18[18:22:22:26] sts knitways. 64[68:78:82:84] sts.

With ws facing, rejoin yarn to rem 64[68:78:82:84] sts and purl to end.

Beg with 1st row of st-st work 4 rows.

Cast off knitways.

### For a Boy

**Next row.** Cast off 18[18:22:22:26] sts knitways, k3[5:5:7:3], k2tog, (k4, k2tog) 11[11:13:13:15] times, k4[6:6:8:4]. 64[68:78:82:84] sts.

Beg with 2nd row of st-st work 5 rows.

Cast off knitways.

### TO MAKE UP

Join side and sleeve seams. Sew back tab in place with a button at either end, across centre of back as illustrated. Sew on buttons, pushing buttons through the fabric of the front borders to create the buttonholes. Pin out coat to the measurement given. Cover with clean, damp tea towels and leave until dry. See ball band for washing and further care instructions.

## Little Garden Coat

Work as given for Little Woodland Coat omitting Neckband and To Make Up.

### NECKBAND

Work from ** to ** as given for Neckband of Little Woodland Coat.

Work 2 rows more in 2x2 rib. Cast off in rib.

### TO MAKE UP

Make Up as given for Little Woodland Coat.

# Little Owl Jersey & Little Owl Hoodie

## MEASUREMENTS

### Ages

| Mths | 0-9 | 9-18 | 18-24 | 3-5 years | 5-7 years |
|---|---|---|---|---|---|
| **To Fit Chest** | | | | | |
| cm | 41-46 | 46-51 | 51-56 | 56-61 | 61-66 |
| in | 16-18 | 18-20 | 20-22 | 22-24 | 24-26 |
| **Actual Measurement** | | | | | |
| cm | 50 | 55 | 61 | 67 | 73 |
| in | 19¾ | 21¾ | 24 | 26½ | 28¾ |
| **Full Length** | | | | | |
| cm | 28 | 32 | 38 | 42 | 48 |
| in | 11 | 12½ | 15 | 16½ | 19 |
| **Sleeve Length** | | | | | |
| cm | 16 | 19 | 23 | 28 | 32 |
| in | 6¼ | 7½ | 9 | 11 | 12½ |

## MATERIALS

**Little Owl Jersey**  Merino Blend DK

| | | | | | | |
|---|---|---|---|---|---|---|
| 854 Fern (A) | | 3A | 3A | 4A | 5A | 6A |
| **Baby Alpaca DK** | | | | | | |
| 697 Rust (B) | 50g | 1 B | 1 B | 1 B | 1 B | 1 B |
| 501 Fawn (C) | balls | 1 C | 1 C | 1 C | 1 C | 1 C |
| 510 Cranberry (D) | | 1 D | 1 D | 1 D | 1 D | 1 D |
| 503 Charcoal (E) | | 1 E | 1 E | 1 E | 1 E | 1 E |

**Little Owl Hoodie**  Baby Alpaca DK

| | | | | | | |
|---|---|---|---|---|---|---|
| 501 Fawn (A) | | 3A | 4A | 5A | 7A | 8A |
| 697 Rust (B) | 50g | 1 B | 1 B | 1 B | 1 B | 1 B |
| 503 Charcoal (C) | balls | 1 C | 1 C | 1 C | 1 C | 1 C |
| 510 Cranberry (D) | | 1 D | 1 D | 1 D | 1 D | 1 D |

Also suitable for any King Cole DK yarns.
It is essential to work to the stated tension to achieve the correct size of garment.

### Needles
1 pair 4 mm (UK 8 – USA 6) knitting needles
1 pair 3¼ mm (UK 10 – USA 3) knitting needles
Stitch holders
2 buttons

### Tension
22 sts and 28 rows to 10 cm, 4 in, over stocking stitch on 4 mm needles or the size required to give the correct tension.

## Little Owl Jersey

**Pattern note:** using a separate ball of wool for each colour, twist the new colour to be used with the colour just finished to prevent a hole forming. This is called **intarsia**.

### DO NOT JOIN IN AND BREAK OFF YARN EXCEPT WHERE NECESSARY

When working patt from chart, work odd numbered rows as knit rows, reading chart from right to left, and even numbered rows as purl rows, reading chart from left to right.

### BACK
Using 3¼ mm needles, thumb method and A, cast on 66[70:78:86:94] sts.
**1st row.** * K2, p2, rep from * to last 2 sts, k2.
**2nd row.** P2, * k2, p2, rep from * to end.
These 2 rows are called **2x2 rib**. Work 5[5:7:7:7] rows more in 2x2 rib.
**Next row.** P7[6:8:6:4], p2tog, (p3[5:4:4:4], p2tog) 10[8:10:12:14] times, p7[6:8:6:4]. 55[61:67:73:79] sts.
Change to 4 mm needles and work as follows:-
**1st row.** Knit.
**2nd row.** Purl.
Last 2 rows form **st-st** (stocking stitch). **
Cont in st-st until back measures 28[32:38:42:48] cm, 11[12½:15:16½:19] in, ending with a ws row.
### Shape Shoulders
Cast off 7[8:10:10:12] sts at beg of next 2 rows. 41[45:47:53:55] sts.
Cast off 8[9:10:11:12] sts at beg of next 2 rows. 25[27:27:31:31] sts.
Leave rem 25[27:27:31:31] sts on a stitch holder.

### FRONT
Work as given for Back to **.
Work 4[10:16:22:30] rows in st-st.
Work as follows:-
**1st row.** K16[19:22:25:28]A, work the next 23 sts as given for 1st row of chart from right to left, k16[19:22:25:28]A.
**2nd row.** P16[19:22:25:28]A, work the next 23 sts as given for 2nd row of chart from left to right, p16[19:22:25:28]A.
1st and 2nd rows set position of chart.
Beg with 3rd row of chart work 32 rows. (using colour E instead of C for the forehead of the owl).
Using A only, cont in st-st until front measures 22[26:31:35:41] cm, 8¾[10¼:12:13¾:16] in, ending with a ws row.
### Shape Neck
*** **Next row.** K20[22:25:26:29], turn, leaving rem 35[39:42:47:50] sts on a stitch holder.
Working on these 20[22:25:26:29] sts only proceed as follows:-
**Next row.** Purl.
Work 2 rows dec 1 st at neck edge in every row. 18[20:23:24:27] sts.

## Chart

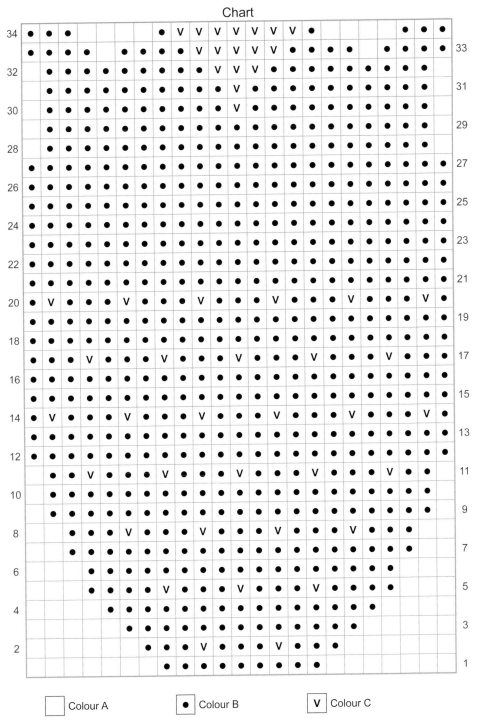

| | Colour A | ● Colour B | V Colour C |

For general information and a key to abbreviations please see page 65

---

sts, purl to end. 8[9:10:11:12] sts.
**Next row.** knit.
Cast off rem 8[9:10:11:12] sts.
***

## SLEEVES (Both alike)
Using 3¼ mm needles,  and thumb method and A, cast on 34[38:38:42:46] sts. Work 7[7:9:9:9] rows in 2x2 rib as given for Back.
**Next row.** P5[4:4:6:4], p2tog, (p9[5:5:5:4], p2tog) 2[4:4:4:6] times, p5[4:4:6:4]. 31[33:33:37:39] sts.
Change to 4 mm needles and work in st-st inc 1 st at each end of 5th and every foll 4th[4th:4th:6th:6th] row to 45[45:47:57:55] sts.
**For 2nd, 3rd and 5th sizes only**
Inc 1 st at each end of every foll [6th:6th:8th] row to [49:53:61] sts.
**For all sizes**
Cont without shaping until sleeve measures 16[19:23:28:32] cm, 6¼[7½:9:11:12½] in, ending with a ws row.
**Shape Sleeve Top**
Cast off 4[4:3:3:3] sts at beg of next 6[2:6:2:6] rows. 21[41:35:51:43] sts.
Cast off 5[5:4:4:4] sts at beg of next 2[6:6:10:8] rows. 11 sts.
Cast off rem 11 sts.

## NECKBAND
Join right shoulder seam.
With rs facing, using 3¼ mm needles and A, pick up and knit 19[19:21:21:21] sts evenly down left side of neck, knit across 15[17:17:21:21] sts left on a stitch holder at front of neck, pick up and knit 19[19:21:21:21] sts evenly up right side of neck and knit across 25[27:27:31:31] sts left on a stitch holder at back of neck. 78[82:86:94:94] sts.
Beg with 2nd row of 2x2 rib as given for Back work 7[7:9:9:9] rows.
Cast off loosely in rib.

---

Work 5 rows dec 1 st at neck edge in next and every foll alt row. 15[17:20:21:24] sts.
Cont without shaping until front measures 28[32:38:42:48] cm, 11[12½:15:16½:19] in, ending with a ws row.
**Shape Shoulder**
**Next row.** Cast off 7[8:10:10:12] sts, knit to end. 8[9:10:11:12] sts.
**Next row.** Purl.
Cast off rem 8[9:10:11:12] sts.
With rs facing, working on rem 35[39:42:47:50] sts left on a stitch holder, slip first

15[17:17:21:21] sts onto a stitch holder, rejoin yarn to rem 20[22:25:26:29] sts, knit to end.
**Next row.** Purl.
Work 2 rows dec 1 st at neck edge in every row. 18[20:23:24:27] sts.
Work 5 rows dec 1 st at neck edge in next and every foll alt row. 15[17:20:21:24] sts.
Cont without shaping until front measures 28[32:38:42:48] cm, 11[12½:15:16½:19] in, ending with a rs row.
**Shape Shoulder**
**Next row.** Cast off 7[8:10:10:12]

## OWL'S BEAK

Using 3¼ mm needles, thumb method and D, cast on 5 sts. Work 2 rows in st-st .
**3rd row.** S1, k1, psso, k1, k2tog. 3 sts.
**4th row.** Purl.
**5th row.** Knit.
**6th row.** Purl.
**7th row.** S1, k2tog, psso. Fasten off.

## TO MAKE UP

Join left shoulder and neckband seams. Fold sleeves in half lengthways, then placing sleeve top folds to shoulder seams, sew sleeves in position for 12[13:14:15:16] cm, 4¾[5¼:5½:6:6¼] in, from top of shoulders. Join side and sleeve seams. Sew on beak to front of jersey as illustrated. Sew on buttons approximately 2 cm, ¾ in at either side of the beak and in line with top of beak. Using C and straight stitch approximately 1 cm in length embroider around the button as illustrated. Using E and straight stitch approximately ½ cm in length embroider around outer eyes as illustrated. Pin out jersey to the measurement given. Cover with clean, damp tea towels and leave until dry. See ball band for washing and further care instructions.

## Little Owl Hoodie

**Pattern note:** using a separate ball of wool for each colour, twist the new colour to be used with the colour just finished to prevent a hole forming. This is called **intarsia**.

## DO NOT JOIN IN AND BREAK OFF YARN EXCEPT WHERE NECESSARY

When working patt from chart, work odd numbered rows as knit rows, reading chart from right to left, and even numbered rows as purl rows, reading chart from left to right.

## BACK

Work as given for Back of Little Owl Jersey.

## FRONT

Work as given for Back of Little Owl Jersey to **.
Work 6[12:18:24:32] rows in st-st.
Work as follows:-
**1st row.** K16[19:22:25:28]A, work the next 23 sts as given for 1st row of chart from right to left, k16[19:22:25:28]A.
**2nd row.** P16[19:22:25:28]A, work the next 23 sts as given for 2nd row of chart from left to right, p16[19:22:25:28]A.
1st and 2nd rows set position of chart.
Beg with 3rd row of chart work 32 rows.
Using A only cont in st-st until front measures 23[27:32:36:42] cm, 9[10¾:12½:14:16½] in, ending with a ws row.
**Shape Neck**
Work from *** to *** as given for Front of Little Owl Jersey, casting off centre 15 [17:17:21:21] sts instead of slipping them onto a stitch holder.

## SLEEVES (Both alike)

Work as given for Sleeves of Little Owl Jersey.

## HOOD

Join shoulder seams. Using 4 mm needles and A, cast on 19[20:22:22:23] sts, using same needles and yarn work across 25[27:27:31:31] sts left on a stitch holder at back of neck as follows:- k2[3:3:5:5], m1, (k4, m1) 5 times, k3[4:4:6:6] and cast on 19[20:22:22:23] sts. 69[73:77:81:83] sts.
Beg with 2nd row of st-st cont until hood measures 18[19:20:21:22] cm,

7[7½:8:8¼:8¾] in, ending with a ws row.
**Shape Top**
**Next row.** Cast off 23[24:26:27:28] sts, k22[24:24:26:26], cast off rem 23[24:26:27:28] sts.
With ws facing, rejoin yarn to rem 23[25:25:27:27] sts and purl to end.
Cont without shaping until hood measures 10[11:11:12:12] cm, 4[4¼:4¼:4¾:4¾] in, from cast off sts, ending with a ws row.
Cast off.
Join side edges at top of hood to 23[24:26:27:28] cast off sts.

## HOOD BORDER

With rs facing, using 3¼ mm needles and A, pick up and knit 46[49:53:54:58] sts evenly up right side of hood, 22[24:24:26:26] sts from 23[25:25:27:27] cast off sts at top of hood and 46[49:53:54:58] sts evenly down left side of hood. 114[122:130:134:142] sts.
Beg with 2nd row of 2x2 rib as given for Back work 8 rows.
Cast off in rib.

## OWL'S BEAK

Work as given for Owl's Beak of Little Owl Jersey.

## TO MAKE UP

Fold sleeves in half lengthways, then placing sleeve top folds to shoulder seams, sew sleeves in position for 12[13:14:15:16] cm, 4¾[5¼:5½:6:6¼] in, from top of shoulders. Join side and sleeve seams. Placing hood borders to centre of front neck, sew hood evenly in position along neck edge gathering in any fullness. Sew on beak to front of hoodie as illustrated. Sew on buttons approximately 2 cm, ¾ in at either side of the beak and in line with top of beak. Using A and straight stitch approximately 1 cm in length embroider around the button as illustrated. Using C and straight stitch approximately ½ cm in length embroider around outer eyes as illustrated. Pin out hoodie to the measurement given. Cover with clean, damp tea towels and leave until dry. See ball band for washing and further care instructions.

# Little Walking Jacket & Little Boating Jacket

## MEASUREMENTS

### Ages

| Mths | 0-9 | 9-18 | 18-24 | 3-4 years | 5-7 years |
|---|---|---|---|---|---|
| **To Fit Chest** | | | | | |
| cm | 41-46 | 46-51 | 51-56 | 56-61 | 61-66 |
| in | 16-18 | 18-20 | 20-22 | 22-24 | 24-26 |
| **Actual Measurement** | | | | | |
| cm | 53 | 58 | 63 | 68 | 73 |
| in | 21 | 22¾ | 24¾ | 26¾ | 28¾ |
| **Full Length** | | | | | |
| cm | 30 | 33 | 37 | 43 | 48 |
| in | 11¾ | 13 | 14½ | 17 | 19 |
| **Sleeve Length** | | | | | |
| cm | 15 | 18 | 22 | 27 | 31 |
| in | 6 | 7 | 8¾ | 10¾ | 12 |

## MATERIALS

### Little Walking Jacket

| | | | | | | |
|---|---|---|---|---|---|---|
| Baby Alpaca DK Shade 505 Sage | 50g balls | 6 | 7 | 9 | 11 | 14 |

### Little Boating Jacket

| | | | | | | |
|---|---|---|---|---|---|---|
| Bamboo Cotton DK shade 635 Lawn | 100g balls | 2 | 3 | 3 | 4 | 5 |

Also suitable for any King Cole DK yarns.
It is essential to work to the stated tension to achieve the correct size of garment.

### Needles
1 pair 4 mm (UK 8 – USA 6) knitting needles
1 pair 3¼ mm (UK 10 – USA 3) knitting needles
6[6:6:7:7] buttons for Coat with Hood and Coat with Collar.

### Tension
22 sts and 40 rows to 10 cm, 4 in, over texture pattern on 4 mm needles or the size required to give the correct tension.

## Little Walking Jacket

### BACK

Using 3¼ mm needles and thumb method cast on 70[74:82:90:94] sts.
**1st row.** * K2, p2, rep from * to last 2 sts, k2.

**2nd row.** P2, * k2, p2, rep from * to end.
These 2 rows are called **2x2 rib**.
Work 7[7:7:9:9] rows more in 2x2 rib.
**Next row.** Rib to end inc 0[2:4:2:4] sts evenly across row. 70[76:86:92:98] sts.
Change to 4 mm needles and work as follows:-
**1st row.** P3[4:3:3:3], * k8, p6[7:4:5:6], rep from * to last 11[12:11:11:11] sts, k8, p3[4:3:3:3].
**2nd row.** K3[4:3:3:3], p8, * k6[7:4:5:6], p8, rep from * to last 3[4:3:3:3] sts, k3[4:3:3:3].
**3rd row.** P3[4:3:3:3], * slip next 4 sts onto CN and hold at back of work, k4 then k4 from CN, this will now be called **C8B**, p6[7:4:5:6], rep from *

to last 11[12:11:11:11] sts, C8B, p3[4:3:3:3].
**4th row.** As 2nd row.
**5th and 6th rows.** As 1st and 2nd rows.
**7th row.** As 1st row.
**8th row.** K3[4:3:3:3], p8, * k6[7:4:5:6], p8, rep from * to last 3[4:3:3:3] sts, k3[4:3:3:3].
From 1st to 8th row forms **cable patt**.
Cont in cable patt until back measures approximately 10[10:13:14:16] cm, 4[4:5¼:5½:6¼] in, ending with 5th row of patt.
**Next row.** Patt 4[7:2:5:8], patt2tog, (patt 4[3:3:3:3], patt2tog) 10[12:16:16:16] times, patt 4[7:2:5:8]. 59[63:69:75:81] sts.
Work as follows:-

**1st row.** Knit.
**2nd row.** Purl.
**3rd row.** K1[1:0:1:0], * p1, k1, rep from * to last 0[0:1:0:1] sts, p0[0:1:0:1].
**4th row.** K0[0:1:0:1], p1, * k1B, p1, rep from * to last 0[0:1:0:1] sts, k0[0:1:0:1].
From 1st to 4th row forms **textured patt**.
Cont in textured patt until back measures 30[33:37:43:48] cm, 11¾[13:14½:17:19] in, ending with a ws row.
**Shape Shoulders**
Cast off 8[9:10:11:12] sts in patt at beg of next 2 rows. 43[45:49:53:57] sts.
Cast off 9[9:11:11:13] sts in patt at beg of next 2 rows. 25[27:27:31:31] sts.
Cast off rem 25[27:27:31:31] sts in patt.

**LEFT FRONT**
Using 3¼ mm needles and thumb method cast on 35[35:39:43:47] sts.
**1st row.** * K2, p2, rep from * to last 3 sts, k2, p1.
**2nd row.** K1, p2, * k2, p2, rep from * to end.
1st and 2nd rows form **rib**.
Work 7[7:7:9:9] rows more in rib.
**Next row.** Rib to end dec 3[0:0:0:1] sts evenly across row for 1st and 5th sizes only and inc 1 st in centre of row for 3rd size only. 32[35:40:43:46] sts.
Change to 4 mm needles and work as follows:-
**1st row.** P3[4:3:3:3], * k8, p6[7:4:5:6], * rep from * to * 1[1:2:2:2] times, p1.
**2nd row.** K1, * k6[7:4:5:6], p8, * rep from * to * 1 [1:2:2:2] times, k3[4:3:3:3].
**3rd row.** P3[4:3:3:3], * C8B, p6[7:4:5:6],* rep from * to * 1 [1:2:2:2] times, p1.
**4th row.** As 2nd row.
**5th and 6th rows.** As 1st and 2nd rows.
**7th row.** As 1st row.

**8th row.** K1, * k6[7:4:5:6], p8, * rep from * to * 1[1:2:2:2] times, k3[4:3:3:3].
From 1st to 8th row forms **cable patt**.
Cont in cable patt until left front measures approximately 10[10:13:14:16] cm, 4[4:5¼:5½:6¼] in, ending with 5th row of patt.
**Next row.** Patt 3[4:5:3:4], patt2tog, (patt 4[3:2:3:3], patt2tog) 4[5:7:7:7] times, patt 3[4:5:3:5]. 27[29:32:35:38] sts.
Work as follows:-
**1st row.** Knit.
**2nd row.** Purl.
**3rd row.** K1[1:0:1:0], * p1, k1, rep from * to end.
**4th row.** P1, * k1B, p1, rep from * to last 0[0:1:0:1] sts, k0[0:1:0:1].
From 1st to 4th row forms **textured patt**.
Cont in textured patt until left front measures 27[30:33:39:44]

cm, 10¾[11¾:13:15½:17¼] in, ending with a rs row.
**Shape Neck**
**Next row.** Cast off 5[6:6:8:8] sts in patt, patt to end. 22[23:26:27:30] sts.
Work 2 rows dec 1 st at neck edge in every row. 20[21:24:25:28] sts.
Work 5 rows dec 1 st at neck edge in next and every foll alt row. 17[18:21:22:25] sts.
Cont without shaping until left front measures 30[33:37:43:48] cm, 11¾[13:14½:17:19] in, ending with a ws row.
**Shape Shoulder**
**Next row.** Cast off 8[9:10:11:12] sts in patt, patt to end. 9[9:11:11:13] sts.
**Next row.** Patt.
Cast off rem 9[9:11:11:13] sts in patt.

**RIGHT FRONT**
Using 3¼ mm needles

and thumb method cast on 35[35:39:43:47] sts.

**1st row.** P1, k2, * p2, k2, rep from * to end.

**2nd row.** * P2, k2, rep from * to last 3 sts, p2, k1.

1st and 2nd rows form **rib**. Work 7[7:7:9:9] rows more in rib.

**Next row.** Rib to end dec 3[0:0:0:1] sts evenly across row for 1st and 5th sizes only and inc 1 st in centre of row for 3rd size only. 32[35:40:43:46] sts. Change to 4 mm needles and work as follows:-

**1st row.** P7[8:5:6:7], * k8, p6[7:4:5:6], * rep from * to * 0[0:1:1:1] times, k8, p3[4:3:3:3].

**2nd row.** K3[4:3:3:3], p8, * k6[7:4:5:6], p8, * rep from * to * 0[0:1:1:1] times, k7[8:5:6:7].

**3rd row.** P7[8:5:6:7], * C8B, p6[7:4:5:6],* rep from * to * 0[0:1:1:1] times, C8B, p3[4:3:3:3].

**4th row.** As 2nd row.

**5th and 6th rows.** As 1st and 2nd rows.

**7th row.** As 1st row.

**8th row.** K3[4:3:3:3], p8, * k6[7:4:5:6], p8, * rep from * to * 0[0:1:1:1] times, k7[8:5:6:7].

From 1st to 8th row forms **cable patt**.

Cont in cable patt until right front measures approximately 10[10:13:14:16] cm, 4[4:5¼:5½:6¼] in, ending with 5th row of patt.

**Next row.** Patt 3[4:5:3:5], patt2tog, (patt 4[3:2:3:3], patt2tog) 4[5:7:7:7] times, patt 3[4:5:3:4]. 27[29:32:35:38] sts.
Work as follows:-

**1st row.** Knit.

**2nd row.** Purl.

**3rd row.** K1, * p1, k1, rep from * to last 0[0:1:0:1] sts, p0[0:1:0:1].

**4th row.** K0[0:1:0:1], p1, * k1B, p1, rep from * to end.

From 1st to 4th row forms **textured patt**.

Cont in textured patt until right front measures 27[30:33:39:44]

cm, 10¾[11¾:13:15½:17¼] in, ending with a ws row.

**Shape Neck**

**Next row.** Cast off 5[6:6:8:8] sts in patt, patt to end. 22[23:26:27:30] sts.

**Next row.** Patt.
Work 2 rows dec 1 st at neck edge in every row. 20[21:24:25:28] sts.
Work 5 rows dec 1 st at neck edge in next and every foll alt row. 17[18:21:22:25] sts.
Cont without shaping until right front measures 30[33:37:43:48] cm, 11¾[13:14½:17:19] in, ending with a rs row.

**Shape Shoulder**

**Next row.** Cast off 8[9:10:11:12] sts in patt, patt to end. 9[9:11:11:13] sts.

**Next row.** Patt.
Cast off rem 9[9:11:11:13] sts in patt.

**SLEEVES (Both alike)**

Using 3¼ mm needles and thumb method cast on 42[42:46:50:54] sts. Work 9[9:9:11:11] rows in 2x2 rib as given for Back.

**Next row.** P5[6:4:3:5], p2tog, (p3[5:4:5:5], p2tog) 6[4:6:6:6] times, p5[6:4:3:5]. 35[37:39:43:47] sts.
Change to 4 mm needles and work as follows:-

**1st row.** Knit.

**2nd row.** Purl.

**3rd row.** K1, * p1, k1, rep from * to end.

**4th row.** P1, * k1B, p1, rep from * to end.

From 1st to 4th row forms **textured patt**.

Cont in textured patt inc 1 st at each end of next and every foll 4th[6th:6th:8th:10th] row to 43[53:47:51:67] sts, working inc sts in patt.

**For 1st, 3rd and 4th sizes only**

Inc 1 st at each end of every foll 6th[8th:10th] row to 49[57:61] sts, working inc sts in patt.

**For all sizes**

Cont without shaping until sleeve measures 15[18:22:27:31] cm, 6[7:8¾:10¾:12] in, ending with a ws row.

**Shape Sleeve Top**

Cast off 2 sts in patt at beg of next 10[6:14:10:16] rows. 29[41:29:41:35] sts.
Cast off 3 sts in patt at beg of next 6[10:6:10:8] rows. 11 sts.
Cast off rem 11 sts in patt.

**RIGHT FRONT BORDER**

With rs facing, using 3¼ mm needles pick up and knit 9[9:9:11:11] sts evenly up rib, 21[21:26:31:35] sts evenly up cable patt and 52[64:67:80:92] sts evenly up remainder of front edge. 82[94:102:122:138] sts.
Beg with 2nd row of 2x2 rib as given for Back work 3[3:3:4:4] rows.

**For a Girl**

**Next row.** Rib 3[4:3:3:2], cast off 1 st, (rib 13[15:17:17:20], cast off 1 st) 5[5:5:6:6] times, rib 2[3:2:3:2].

**Next row.** Rib 3[4:3:4:3], cast on 1 st, (rib 14[16:18:18:21], cast on 1 st) 5[5:5:6:6] times, rib 3[4:3:3:2].
Work 4[4:4:5:5] rows more in 2x2 rib.
Cast off in rib.

**For a Boy**

Work 6[6:6:7:7] rows more in 2x2 rib.
Cast off in rib.

**LEFT FRONT BORDER**

With rs facing, using 3¼ mm needles pick up and knit 52[64:67:80:92] sts evenly down front edge to beg of cable patt, 21[21:26:31:35] sts evenly down cable patt and 9[9:9:11:11] sts evenly down rib. 82[94:102:122:138] sts.
Beg with 2nd row of 2x2 rib as given for Back work 9[9:9:11:11] rows.
Cast off in rib.

## HOOD

Join shoulder seams. Using 4 mm needles cast on 22[23:25:25:26] sts, using same needles and yarn pick up and knit 31[33:33:35:37] sts from 25[27:27:31:31] cast off sts at back of neck and cast on 22[23:25:25:26] sts. 75[79:83:85:89] sts.
Beg with 2nd of texture patt as given for Back cont until hood measures 19[20:21:22:23] cm, 7½[8:8¼:8¾:9] in, ending with a ws row.

### Shape Top

**Next Row.** Cast off 25[26:27:28:30] sts, in patt, patt 24[26:28:28:28], cast off rem 25[26:27:28:30] sts in patt.
With ws facing, rejoin yarn to rem 25[27:29:29:29] sts and patt to end.
Cont without shaping until hood measures 11[12:12:13:14] cm, 4¼[4¾:4¾:5¼:5½] in, from cast off sts, ending with a ws row.
Cast off in patt.
Join side edges at top of hood to 25[26:27:28:30] cast off sts.

## HOOD BORDER

With rs facing, using 3¼ mm needles pick up and knit 60[64:68:72:76] sts evenly up right side of hood, 26[26:30:30:30] sts from 25[27:29:29:29] cast off sts at top of hood and 60[64:68:72:76] sts evenly down left side of hood. 146[154:166:174:182] sts.
Beg with 2nd row of 2x2 rib as given for Back work 10[10:10:12:12] rows.
Cast off in rib.

## EARS (Make 4 pieces)

Using 4 mm needles and thumb method cast on 12 sts.
**1st row.** Knit.
**2nd row.** Purl.
Last 2 rows form **st-st** (stocking stitch).
Work in st-st throughout as follows:-
Work 4 rows, ending with a ws row. Dec 1 st at each end of next and foll alt row, then on foll row, ending with a ws row. Cast off rem 6 sts.

## TO MAKE UP

Fold sleeves in half lengthways, then placing sleeve top folds to shoulder seams, sew sleeves in position for approximately 12[13:14:15:16] cm, 4¾[5¼:5½:6:6¼] in, from top of shoulders. Join side and sleeve seams. Placing hood borders halfway across front borders, sew hood evenly in position along neck edge gathering in any fullness. Sew 2 pieces together to form ears and sew to top of hood. Sew on buttons. Pin out jacket to the measurement given. Cover with clean, damp tea towels and leave until dry. See ball band for washing and further care instructions.

~~~~~~~~~~~~~~~~~~~~~~~~~~~~~~~~

## Little Boating Jacket

Work as given for Little Walking jacket omitting Front Borders, Hood, Hood Border, Ears and To Make Up.

## RIGHT FRONT BORDER

With rs facing, using 3¼ mm needles pick up and knit 9[9:9:11:11] sts evenly up rib, 21[21:26:31:35] sts evenly up cable patt and 52[64:67:80:92] sts evenly up remainder of front edge. 82[94:102:122:138] sts.
Beg with 2nd row of 2x2 rib as given for Back work 3[3:3:4:4] rows.

### For a Girl

**Next row.** Rib 3[4:3:3:2], cast off 1 st, (rib 13[15:17:17:20], cast off 1 st) 5[5:5:6:6] times, rib 2[3:2:3:2].
**Next row.** Rib 3[4:3:4:3], cast on 1 st, (rib 14[16:18:18:21], cast on 1 st) 5[5:5:6:6] times, rib 3[4:3:3:2].
Work 4[4:4:5:5] rows more in 2x2 rib.
Cast off in rib.

### For a Boy

Work 6[6:6:7:7] rows more in 2x2 rib.
Cast off in rib.

## LEFT FRONT BORDER

With rs facing, using 3¼ mm needles pick up and knit 52[64:67:80:92] sts evenly down front edge to beg of cable patt, 21[21:26:31:35] sts evenly down cable patt and 9[9:9:11:11] sts evenly down rib. 82[94:102:122:138] sts.
Beg with 2nd row of 2x2 rib as given for Back work 3[3:3:4:4] rows.

### For a Boy

**Next row.** Rib 3[4:3:4:3], cast off 1 st, (rib 13[15:17:17:20], cast off 1 st) 5[5:5:6:6] times, rib 2[3:2:2:1].
**Next row.** Rib 3[4:3:3:2], cast on 1 st, (rib 14[16:18:18:21], cast on 1 st) 5[5:5:6:6] times, rib 3[4:3:4:3].
Work 4[4:4:5:5] rows more in 2x2 rib.
Cast off in rib.

### For a Girl

Work 6[6:6:7:7] rows more in 2x2 rib.
Cast off in rib.

## COLLAR

Join shoulder seams. With rs facing, using 3¼ mm needles and beg halfway across right front border pick up and knit 20[21:25:27:27] sts evenly up right side of neck, 30[32:32:36:36] sts from 25[27:27:31:31] cast off sts at back of neck and 20[21:25:27:27] sts evenly down left side of neck 70[74:82:90:90] sts.
Beg with 1st row of 2x2 rib as given for Back work for 6[6:7:7:7] cm, 2½[2½:2¾:2¾:2¾] in, ending with 1st row of rib.

**Next row.** Rib 14[14:18:18:18], k1, m1, k1, (p2, k1, m1,k1) 10[11:11:13:13] times, rib 14[14:18:18:18]. 81[86:94:104:104] sts.
**Next row.** Rib 14[14:18:18:18], (p3, k2) 10[11:11:13:13] times, p3, rib 14[14:18:18:18].
Cast off in rib.
**TO MAKE UP**
Fold sleeves in half lengthways, then placing sleeve top folds to shoulder seams, sew sleeves in position for approximately 12[13:14:15:16] cm,

4¾[5¼:5½:6:6¼] in, from top of shoulders. Join side and sleeve seams. Sew on buttons. Pin out jacket to the measurement given. Cover with clean, damp tea towels and leave until dry. See ball band for washing and further care instructions.

# Little Owl Hat, Little Petal Hat, Funny Bunny Hat, Little Star Hat, Little Cub Hat, & Foxy Hat

## MEASUREMENTS
### To Fit Age (approx)

| Mths | 6-12 | 1-2 yrs | 2-3 yrs | 4-5 yrs | 6-7 yrs |
|---|---|---|---|---|---|
| **Little Owl Hat** | | | | | |
| Width Around Head | | | | | |
| cm | 36 | 38 | 41 | 42 | 44 |
| in | 14 | 15 | 16 | 16½ | 17¼ |
| **Little Petal Hat, Funny Bunny Hat and Little Star Hat** | | | | | |
| Width Around Head | | | | | |
| cm | 36 | 39 | 41 | 41 | 44 |
| in | 14 | 15½ | 16 | 16 | 17¼ |
| **Little Cub Hat** | | | | | |
| Width Around Head | | | | | |
| cm | 37 | 40 | 43 | 43 | 46 |
| in | 14½ | 15¾ | 17 | 17 | 18 |
| **Foxy Hat** | | | | | |
| Width Around Head | | | | | |
| cm | 35 | 37 | 41 | 43 | 45 |
| in | 13¾ | 14½ | 16 | 17 | 17¾ |

## MATERIALS

**Little Owl Hat**  Baby Alpaca Dk

| | | | | | | |
|---|---|---|---|---|---|---|
| M - 697 Rust | | 1M | 1M | 1M | 2M | 2M |
| A - 503 Charcoal | 50g | 1A | 1A | 1A | 1A | 1A |
| B - 510 Cranberry | balls | 1B | 1B | 1B | 1B | 1B |
| C - 501 Fawn | | 1C | 1C | 1C | 1C | 1C |

**Little Petal Hat**  Cottonsoft  Dk

| | | | | | | |
|---|---|---|---|---|---|---|
| M - 712 Rose | 100g | 1M | 1M | 1M | 1M | 1M |
| C - 710 White | balls | 1C | 1C | 1C | 1C | 1C |

**Little Cub Hat**  Baby Alpaca Dk

| | | | | | | |
|---|---|---|---|---|---|---|
| Shade 504 Koala | 50g balls | 1 | 1 | 2 | 2 | 2 |

**Funny Bunny Hat**  Baby Alpaca Dk

| | | | | | | |
|---|---|---|---|---|---|---|
| M - 502 Grey | 50g | 1M | 1M | 2M | 2M | 2M |
| C - 501 Fawn | balls | 1C | 1C | 1C | 1C | 1C |

**Little Star Hat**  Bamboo Cotton Dk

| | | | | | | |
|---|---|---|---|---|---|---|
| M - 525 Cobalt | 100g | 1M | 1M | 1M | 1M | 1M |
| C - 634 Crimson | balls | 1C | 1C | 1C | 1C | 1C |

**Foxy Hat**  King Cole Baby Alpaca Dk

| | | | | | | |
|---|---|---|---|---|---|---|
| M - 697 Rust | 50g balls | 1M | 1M | 1M | 1M | 1M |
| A – 501 Fawn | | 1A | 1A | 1A | 1A | 1A |
| B - 503 Charcoal | | 1C | 1C | 1C | 1C | 1C |

**Needles**
1 pair 3¼mm (UK 10 – USA 3) knitting needles
1 pair 4mm (UK 8 – USA 6) knitting needles
Owl Hat  2 buttons

**Tension**
22 sts and 28 rows to 10cm, 4in, over stocking stitch on 4mm needles or the size required to give the correct tension.

## Little Owl Hat

### MAIN SECTION
Using 3¼ mm needles, M and thumb method cast on 93[99:107:109:115] sts.
**1st row.** K1, * p1, k1, rep from * to end.
**2nd row.** P1, * k1, p1, rep from * to end.
These 2 rows form **1x1 rib**.
Work in 1x1 rib for a further 7 rows, ending with a **rs** row.
**10th row.** Rib 1[2:2:3:4], (rib 2, work2tog, rib 5[4:5:5:4], work2tog, rib 2) 7[8:8:8:9] times, rib 1[1:1:2:3]. 79[83:91:93:97] sts.
Change to 4 mm needles.
Joining in A as required and stranding yarn not in use loosely across ws of work, now work in patt as follows:-
**1st row.** With M, knit.
**2nd row.** Purl 3[3:3:2:2]M, * 1A, 3M, rep from * to last 0[0:0:3:3] sts, (1A, 2M) 0[0:0:1:1] times.
**3rd row.** With M, knit.
**4th row.** With M, purl.
**5th row.** Knit 1[1:1:0:0]M, * 1A, 3M,  rep from * to last 2[2:2:1:1] sts, 1A, 1[1:1:0:0]M.
**6th row.** With M, purl.
These 6 rows form **patt**.
Work in patt for a further 8[8:8:12:12] rows, ending with a ws row.
Break off A and cont using M

only.
**Next row.** Knit.
**Next row.** Purl.
These 2 rows form **st-st** (stocking stitch).
Cont in st-st until Hat measures 18[19:19:20:20] cm, 7[7½:7½:8:8] in, ending with a ws row.
Cast off.

## BEAK
Using 4 mm needles, B and thumb method cast on 7 sts.
**1st row.** Knit.
**2nd row.** Purl.
**3rd row.** Sl 1, k1, psso, k3, k2tog. 5 sts.
**4th row.** Purl.
**5th and 6th rows.** As 1st and 2nd rows.
**7th row.** Sl 1, k1, psso, k1, k2tog. 3 sts.
**8th row.** Purl.
**9th row.** Sl 1, k2tog, psso and fasten off.

## TO MAKE UP
Using photograph as a guide, sew cast-on edge of Beak to centre of Hat 3 cm (1¼ in) above last row of patt using B. Using C, attach buttons to Hat either side and slightly above cast-on edge of Beak. Now embroider around buttons to form eyes as follows: Using C, embroider a ring of straight stitches, each 1 cm (  in) long, radiating out from edge of button. Now using A embroider another ring of straight stitches, each 5 mm (¼ in) long, outside ring of stitches in C.
Join row-end edges to form a tube. Fold tube flat so that seam runs along centre of tube and join cast-off edges (to form top seam of Hat). Using M, A, B and C, make two 5 cm (2 in) diameter pompons and attach one to each end of top seam of Hat.
Pin out Hat to the measurements given. Cover

with clean, damp tea towels and leave to dry. See ball band for washing and further care instructions.

# Little Petal Hat

## MAIN SECTION
Using 3¼ mm needles, M and thumb method cast on 79[85:91:91:97] sts.
**1st row.** Knit.
**2nd row.** Purl.
These 2 rows form **st-st** (stocking stitch).
Work in st-st for a further 2 rows, ending with a ws row.
Change to 4mm needles.
Work a further 18[20:20:20:20] rows, ending with a ws row.
Break off M and join in C.
Work 8[8:6:8:6] rows, ending with a ws row.
**Shape Top**
**For 5th size only**
**Next row.** (K14, k2tog) 6 times, k1. 91 sts.
Work 1 row.
**For 3rd, 4th and 5th size only**
**Next row.** (K13, k2tog) 6 times, k1. 85 sts.
Work 1 row.
**For 2nd, 3rd, 4th and 5th size only**
**Next row.** (K12, k2tog) 6 times, k1. 79 sts.
Work 1 row.

**For all sizes**
**1st row.** (K11, k2tog) 6 times, k1. 73 sts.
Work 1 row.
**3rd row.** (K10, k2tog) 6 times, k1. 67 sts.
Work 1 row.
**5th row.** (K9, k2tog) 6 times, k1. 61 sts.
Work 1 row.
**7th row.** (K8, k2tog) 6 times, k1. 55 sts.
**8th row.** P1, (p2tog, p7) 6 times. 49 sts.
**9th row.** (K6, k2tog) 6 times, k1. 43 sts.
**10th row.** P1, (p2tog, p5) 6 times. 37 sts.
**11th row.** (K4, k2tog) 6 times, k1. 31 sts.
**12th row.** P1, (p2tog, p3) 6 times. 25 sts.
**13th row.** (K2, k2tog) 6 times, k1. 19 sts.
**14th row.** P1, (p2tog, p1) 6 times. 13 sts.
Change to 3¼ mm needles.
**15th row.** (K2tog, k1) 3 times, (k2tog) twice. 8 sts.
**16th row.** Purl.
**17th row.** Knit.
Rep last 2 rows once more, ending with a rs row.
Break yarn and thread through rem 8 sts. Pull up tightly and fasten off securely.

## TO MAKE UP
Join back seam.
Pin out Hat to the measurements given. Cover with clean, damp tea towels and leave to dry. See ball band for washing and further care instructions.

# Little Cub Hat

## TENSION
20 sts and 40 rows to 10 cm, 4 in, over pattern on 4 mm needles or the size required to give the correct tension.

## MAIN SECTION

Using 3¼ mm needles and thumb method cast on 94[102:110:110:114] sts.
**1st row.** K2, * p2, k2, rep from * to end.
**2nd row.** P2, * k2, p2, rep from * to end.

These 2 rows form **2x2 rib**. Work in 2x2 rib for a further 7 rows, ending with a rs row.
**10th row.** Rib 1[1:0:0:7], work 2 tog, (rib 3, work 2 tog, rib 2, work 2 tog) 10[11:12:12:11] times, rib 1[0:0:0:6]. 73[79:85:85:91] sts.
Change to 4mm needles. Now work in patt as follows:
**1st row.** Knit.
**2nd row.** Purl.
**3rd row.** K1, * p1, k1, rep from * to end.
**4th row.** P1, * k1 below, p1, rep from * to end.
These 4 rows form **patt**.
Work in patt for a further 30[34:34:38:38] rows, ending after 2nd patt row and with a ws row.
**Shape Top**
**1st row.** * (K1, p1) twice, k2tog, rep from * to last st, k1. 61[66:71:71:76] sts.
**2nd row.** P1, * (p1, k1 below) twice, p1, rep from * to end.
**3rd row.** Knit.

**4th row.** Purl.
**5th row.** * (K1, p1) twice, k1, rep from * to last st, k1.
**6th row.** As 2nd row.
**7th row.** (K3, k2tog) 12[13:14:14:15] times, k1. 49[53:57:57:61] sts.
**8th row.** Purl.
**9th row.** K1, * p1, k1, rep from * to end.
**10th row.** P1, * k1 below, p1, rep from * to end.
**11th row.** (K2, k2tog) 12[13:14:14:15] times, k1. 37[40:43:43:46] sts.
**12th row.** Purl.
**13th row.** (K1, p1, k1) 12[13:14:14:15] times, k1.
**14th row.** P1, (p1, k1 below, p1) 12[13:14:14:15] times.
**15th row.** (K1, k2tog) 12[13:14:14:15] times, k1. 25[27:29:29:31] sts.
**16th to 18th rows.** As 8th to 10th rows.
**19th row.** (K2tog) 12[13:14:14:15] times, k1. 13[14:15:15:16] sts.
**20th row.** P1[0:1:1:0], (p2tog) 6[7:7:7:8] times.
Break yarn and thread through rem 7[7:8:8:8] sts. Pull up tightly and fasten off securely.

**EAR PIECES (Make 4)**
Using 4 mm needles and thumb method cast on 12 sts.
**1st row.** Knit.
**2nd row.** Purl.
**3rd to 6th rows.** As 1st and 2nd rows, twice.
**7th row.** K1, sl 1, k1, psso, k6, k2tog, k1. 10 sts.
**8th row.** Purl.
**9th row.** K1, sl 1, k1, psso, k4, k2tog, k1. 8 sts.
**10th row.** P1, p2tog, p2, p2togtbl, p1. 6 sts.
Cast off.

**TO MAKE UP**
Join back seam of Main Section. Sew pairs of Ear Pieces together, leaving cast-on edges open. Using photograph as a guide and gathering base (cast-on edges) of Ears slightly, sew Ears to top of Hat.
Pin out Hat to the measurements given. Cover with clean, damp tea towels and leave to dry. See ball band for washing and further care instructions.

## Funny Bunny Hat

**MAIN SECTION**
Using 3¼ mm needles, M and thumb method cast on 90[98:106:106:114] sts.
**1st row.** K2, * p2, k2, rep from * to end.
**2nd row.** P2, * k2, p2, rep from * to end.
These 2 rows form **2x2 rib**.
Work in 2x2 rib for a further 7 rows, ending with a rs row.
**10th row.** Rib 4[0:3:3:0], work2tog, (rib 6[6:5:5:5], work2tog) 10[12:14:14:16] times, rib 4[0:3:3:0]. 79[85:91:91:97] sts.
Change to 4 mm needles.
**1st row.** Knit.
**2nd row.** Purl.
These 2 rows form **st-st** (stocking stitch).
Work in st-st for a further 20[22:20:22:20] rows, ending

with a ws row.
**Shape Top**
**For 5th size only**
**Next row.** (K14, k2tog) 6 times, k1. 91 sts.
Work 1 row.
**For 3rd, 4th and 5thsize only**
**Next row.** (K13, k2tog) 6 times, k1. 85 sts.
Work 1 row.
**For 2nd, 3rd, 4th and 5th size only**
**Next row.** (K12, k2tog) 6 times, k1. 79 sts.
Work 1 row.
**For all sizes**
**1st row.** (K11, k2tog) 6 times, k1. 73 sts.
Work 1 row.
**3rd row.** (K10, k2tog) 6 times, k1. 67 sts.
Work 1 row.
**5th row.** (K9, k2tog) 6 times, k1. 61 sts.
Work 1 row.
**7th row.** (K8, k2tog) 6 times, k1. 55 sts.
**8th row.** P1, (p2tog, p7) 6 times. 49 sts.
**9th row.** (K6, k2tog) 6 times, k1. 43 sts.
**10th row.** P1, (p2tog, p5) 6 times. 37 sts.
**11th row.** (K4, k2tog) 6 times, k1. 31 sts.
**12th row.** P1, (p2tog, p3) 6 times. 25 sts.
**13th row.** (K2, k2tog) 6 times, k1. 19 sts.
**14th row.** P1, (p2tog, p1) 6 times. 13 sts.
**15th row.** (K2tog, k1) 3 times, (k2tog) twice. 8 sts.
Break yarn and thread through rem 8 sts. Pull up tightly and fasten off securely.

**EAR PIECES (Make 2 in M and 2 in C)**
Using 3¼ mm needles and thumb method cast on 7 sts.
**1st row.** Knit.
**2nd row.** Purl.
These 2 rows form **st-st** (stocking stitch).

Working in st-st (throughout), cont as follows:
**3rd row.** K1, inc in next st, k to last 3 sts, inc in next st, k2. 9 sts.
Work 5 rows.
**9th row.** As 3rd row. 11 sts.
Work 5 rows.
**15th row.** As 3rd row. 13 sts.
Work 7 rows.
**23rd row.** K1, sl 1, k1, psso, k to last 3 sts, k2tog, k1. 11 sts.
Work 5 rows.
**29th row.** As 23rd row. 9 sts.
Work 3 rows.
**33rd row.** As 23rd row. 7 sts.
Work 1 row.
**35th row.** As 23rd row. 5 sts.
**36th row.** P1, p3tog, p1. 3 sts.
**37th row.** Sl 1, k2tog, psso and fasten off.

## TO MAKE UP
Join back seam of Main Section. Sew one of each colour of Ear Pieces together, leaving cast-on edges open. Using photograph as a guide and gathering base (cast-on edges) of Ears slightly, sew Ears to top of Hat. Pin out Hat to the measurements given. Cover with clean, damp tea towels and leave to dry. See ball band for washing and further care instructions.

Little Star Hat

## MAIN SECTION
Using 3¼ mm needles, M and thumb method cast on 79[85:91:91:97] sts.
**1st row.** Knit.
**2nd row.** Purl.
These 2 rows form **st-st** (stocking stitch).
Work in st-st for a further 2 rows, ending with a ws row.
Change to 4mm needles.
Work 2 rows, ending with a ws row.
Using a separate ball of yarn for each block of colour and twisting yarns together where they meet to avoid holes forming, now work star motif as follows:
**1st row.** Knit 39[42:45:45:48]M, 1C, 39[42:45:45:48]M.
**2nd row.** Purl 39[42:45:45:48]M, 1C, 39[42:45:45:48]M.
**3rd row.** Knit 38[41:44:44:47]M, 3C, 38[41:44:44:47]M.
**4th row.** Purl 38[41:44:44:47]M, 3C, 38[41:44:44:47]M.
**5th row.** Knit 37[40:43:43:46]M, 5C, 37[40:43:43:46]M.
**6th row.** Purl 37[40:43:43:46]M, 5C, 37[40:43:43:46]M.
**7th row.** Knit 32[35:38:38:41]M, 15C, 32[35:38:38:41]M.
**8th row.** Purl 32[35:38:38:41]M, 15C, 32[35:38:38:41]M.
**9th row.** Knit 33[36:39:39:42]M, 13C, 33[36:39:39:42]M.
**10th row.** Purl 33[36:39:39:42] M, 13C, 33[36:39:39:42]M.
**11th row.** Knit 34[37:40:40:43] M, 11C, 34[37:40:40:43]M.
**12th row.** Purl 34[37:40:40:43] M, 11C, 34[37:40:40:43]M.
**13th and 14th rows.** As 9th and 10th rows.
**15th and 16th rows.** As 7th and 8th rows.
**17th and 18th rows.** As 5th and 6th rows.
**19th and 20th rows.** As 3rd and 4th rows.
**21st and 22nd rows.** As 1st and 2nd rows.
Break off C and cont using M only.

Work 2[4:2:4:2] rows, ending with a ws row.
Complete as given for Funny Bunny Hat from Shape Top.

## TO MAKE UP
Join back seam.
Pin out Hat to the measurements given. Cover with clean, damp tea towels and leave to dry. See ball band for washing and further care instructions.

# Foxy Hat
## MAIN SECTION
Using 3¼ mm needles, A and thumb method cast on 39[41:45:47:49] sts.
Using a separate ball of yarn for each block of colour and twisting yarns together where they meet to avoid holes forming, work as follows:
**1st row**. Knit 19[20:22:23:24]A, 1M, 19[20:22:23:24]A.
**2nd row**. Purl 18[19:21:22:23]A, 3M, 18[19:21:22:23]A.
**3rd row**. Knit 17[18:20:21:22]A, 5M, 17[18:20:21:22]A.
**4th row**. Purl 17[18:20:21:22]A, 5M, 17[18:20:21:22]A.
Change to 4mm needles.
**5th row**. Knit 16[17:19:20:21]A, 7M, 16[17:19:20:21]A.
**6th row**. Purl 15[16:18:19:20]A, 9M, 15[16:18:19:20]A.

**7th row**. Knit 14[15:17:18:19]A, 11M, 14[15:17:18:19]A.
**8th row**. Purl 14[15:17:18:19]A, 11M, 14[15:17:18:19]A.
**9th row**. Knit 13[14:16:17:18]A, 13M, 13[14:16:17:18]A.
**10th row**. Purl 12[13:15:16:17]A, 15M, 12[13:15:16:17]A.
**11th row**. Knit 11[12:14:15:16]A, 17M, 11[12:14:15:16]A.
**12th row**. Purl 11[12:14:15:16]A, 17M, 11[12:14:15:16]A.
**13th row**. Knit 10[11:13:14:15]A, 19M, 10[11:13:14:15]A.
**14th row**. Purl 9[10:12:13:14]A, 21M, 9[10:12:13:14]A.
**15th row**. Knit 8[9:11:12:13]A, 23M, 8[9:11:12:13]A.
**16th row**. Purl 8[9:11:12:13]A, 23M, 8[9:11:12:13]A.
**17th row**. Knit 7[8:10:11:12]A, 25M, 7[8:10:11:12]A.
**18th row**. Purl 6[7:9:10:11]A, 27M, 6[7:9:10:11]A.
**19th row**. Knit 5[6:8:9:10]A, 29M, 5[6:8:9:10]A.
**20th row**. Purl 5[6:8:9:10]A, 29M, 5[6:8:9:10]A.
**21st row**. Knit 4[5:7:8:9]A, 31M, 4[5:7:8:9]A.
**22nd row**. Purl 3[4:6:7:8]A, 33M, 3[4:6:7:8]A.
**23rd row**. Knit 2[3:5:6:7]A, 35M, 2[3:5:6:7]A.
**24th row**. Purl 2[3:5:6:7]A, 35M, 2[3:5:6:7]A.
**25th row**. Knit 1[2:4:5:6]A, 37M, 1[2:4:5:6]A.
**26th row**. Purl 0[1:3:4:5]A, 39M, 0[1:3:4:5]A.
**For 3rd, 4th and 5th size only**
**27th row**. Knit [2:3:4]A, 41M, [2:3:4]A.
**28th row**. Purl [2:3:4]A, 41M, [2:3:4]A.
**29th row**. Knit [1:2:3]A, 43M, [1:2:3]A.
**30th row**. Purl [0:1:2]A, 45M, [0:1:2]A.
**For 5th size only**
**31st row**. Knit 1A, 47M, 1A.
**32nd row**. Purl 1A, 47M, 1A.
**For all sizes**
Break off A and cont using M only.

**Next row**. Knit.
**Next row**. Purl.
These 2 rows form **st-st** (stocking stitch).
Work in st-st for a further 22[26:22:24:22] rows, ending with a ws row.
Place markers at both ends of last row (to denote fold line for top of Hat).
Work 46[50:50:52:52] rows, ending with a ws row.
Change to 3¼ mm needles.
Work a further 4 rows, ending with a ws row.
Cast off.

## NOSE
Using 3¼ mm needles, B and thumb method cast on 3 sts.
**1st row**. Knit.
**2nd row**. Inc purlwise in first st, p1, inc purlwise in last st. 5 sts.
**3rd row**. Knit.
**4th row**. Inc purlwise in first st, p3, inc purlwise in last st. 7 sts.
**5th row**. Knit.
**6th row**. Purl.
**7th row**. Knit.
**8th row**. P2tog, p3, p2tog. 5 sts.
**9th row**. Knit.
**10th row**. P2tog, p1, p2tog.
Cast off rem 3 sts, leaving a fairly long end.

## STRINGS (Make 2)
Using 3¼ mm needles, M and thumb method cast on 23[24:25:26:27] sts.
**1st row**. Knit.
Cast off knitwise.

## TO MAKE UP
Fold Main Section in half along row indicated by fold line markers and join row-end edges to form side seams.
Lay Hat flat and mark points along side seams and fold at top of Hat approx 5[5:5:6:6] cm, 2[2:2:2½:2½] in, away from corner point. Using photograph as a guide and back stitch, sew through both layers diagonally across corners of Hat between

these marked points to form ears. Using end of yarn, run a gathering thread around outer edge of Nose and pull up to form a ball shape, inserting a few strands of yarn to fill out Nose. Fasten off securely,

then sew Nose to front of Hat as in photograph. Using B and photograph as a guide, embroidery satin stitch eyes on front above and either side of Nose. Attach Strings to base of side seams as in photograph.

Pin out Hat to the measurements given. Cover with clean, damp tea towels and leave to dry. See ball band for washing and further care instructions.

# Little Star Blanket, Little Snowflake Blanket & Little Holiday Blanket

## MEASUREMENTS

**Little Star Blanket**
Width x Length (approximately) — 66 x 72 cm / 26 x 28¼ in

**Little Snowflake Blanket**
Width x Length (approximately) — 66 x 70 cm / 26 x 27½ in

**Little Holiday Blanket**
Width x Length (approximately) — 66 x 76 cm / 26 x 30 in

## MATERIALS

**Little Star Blanket** Bamboo Cotton DK

| | | |
|---|---|---|
| Colour A 634 Crimson | | 1A |
| Colour B 525 Cobalt | 100g balls | 2B |
| Colour C 543 Oyster | | 1C |

**Little Snowflake Blanket** Merino Blend DK

| | | |
|---|---|---|
| Colour A 46 Aran | 50g balls | 3A |
| Colour B 703 Cranberry | | 5B |

**Little Holiday Blanket** Cottonsoft DK

| | | |
|---|---|---|
| 712 Rose | 100g balls | 3 |

Also suitable for any King Cole DK yarns.
It is essential to work to the stated tension to achieve the correct size of garment.

**Needles**
1 pair 4 mm (USA 6 - UK 8) knitting needles
1 pair of 3¼ mm (USA 3 - UK 10) knitting needles

**Tension**
See tension at the beginning of each pattern.

## Little Star Blanket

### TENSION
22 sts and 28 rows to 10 cm, 4 in, over stocking stitch on 4 mm needles, or the size required to give correct tension.

**Pattern note:** using a separate ball of wool for each colour, twist the new colour to be used with the colour just finished to prevent a hole forming. This is called **intarsia.**

**DO NOT JOIN IN AND BREAK OFF YARN EXCEPT WHERE NECESSARY**
Using 3¼ mm needles, colour A and thumb method cast on 148 sts.
**1st row.** P1, k2, * p2, k2, rep from * to last st, p1.
**2nd row.** K1, * p2, k2, rep from * to last 3 sts, p2, k1.
These 2 rows form **rib.**
Work 11 rows more in rib.
**14th row.** P7, p2tog, (p4, p2tog) 22 times, p7. 125 sts.
Change to 4 mm needles and using B, work as follows:-
**1st row.** Knit.
**2nd row.** Purl.
Last 2 rows form **st-st**

(stocking stitch).
Cont in st-st until blanket measures 21.5 cm, 8½ in, ending with a ws row.
Using C, work 18 rows in st-st.

Work as follows:-
**1st row.** K62C, 1A, 62C.
**2nd row.** P62C, 1A, 62C.
**3rd row.** K61C, 3A, 61C.
**4th row.** P61C, 3A, 61C.
**5th row.** K60C, 5A, 60C.
**6th row.** P60C, 5A, 60C.
**7th row.** K59C, 7A, 59C.
**8th row.** P59C, 7A, 59C.
**9th row.** K58C, 9A, 58C.
**10th row.** P58C, 9A, 58C.
**11th row.** K51C, 23A, 51C.
**12th row.** P51C, 23A, 51C.
**13th row.** K52C, 21A, 52C.
**14th row.** P52C, 21A, 52C.
**15th row.** K53C, 19A, 53C.
**16th row.** P53C, 19A, 53C.
**17th row.** K54C, 17A, 54C.
**18th row.** P54C, 17A, 54C.

**19th row.** K55C, 15A, 55C.

**20th row.** P55C, 15A, 55C.

**21st and 22nd rows.** As 17th and 18th rows.

**23rd and 24th rows.** As 15th and 16th rows.

**25th and 26th rows.** As 13th and 14th rows.

**27th and 28th rows.** As 11th and 12th rows.

**29th and 30th rows.** As 9th and 10th rows.

**31st and 32nd rows.** As 7th and 8th rows.

**33rd and 34th rows.** As 5th and 6th rows.

**35th and 36th rows.** As 3rd and 4th rows.

**37th and 38th rows.** As 1st and 2nd rows.

Using C, only work 18 rows in st-st.

Using B, cont in st-st until blanket measures 67 cm, 26½ in, ending with a rs row.

**Next row.** P7, m1, (p5, m1) 22 times, p8. 148 sts.

Change to 3¼ mm needles and using A, work 14 rows in rib. Cast off in rib.

## SIDE BORDERS (Both alike)

With rs facing, using 3¼ mm needles pick up and knit 12 sts evenly along rib, 170 sts evenly along side edge and 12 sts evenly along rib. 194 sts.

**1st row.** * P2, k2, rep from * to last 2 sts, p2.

**2nd row.** K2, * p2, k2, rep from * to end.

These 2 rows form **rib**.

Work 12 rows more in rib. Cast off in rib.

## TO COMPLETE

Pin out blanket to the measurement given. Cover with clean, damp tea towels and leave until dry. See ball band for washing and further care instructions.

## Little Snowflake Blanket

22 sts and 28 rows to 10 cm, 4 in, over stocking stitch on 4 mm needles, or the size required to give correct tension.

### FAIRISLE TECHNIQUE

When working with more than one colour the colour not being used should be twisted around colour being used and stranded loosely across back of work.

When working patt from chart, work odd numbered rows as knit rows, reading chart from right to left, and even numbered rows as purl rows, reading chart from left to right.

Using 3¼ mm needles, colour A and thumb method cast on 148 sts.

**1st row.** P1, k2, * p2, k2, rep from * to last st, p1.

**2nd row.** K1, * p2, k2, rep from * to last 3 sts, p2, k1.

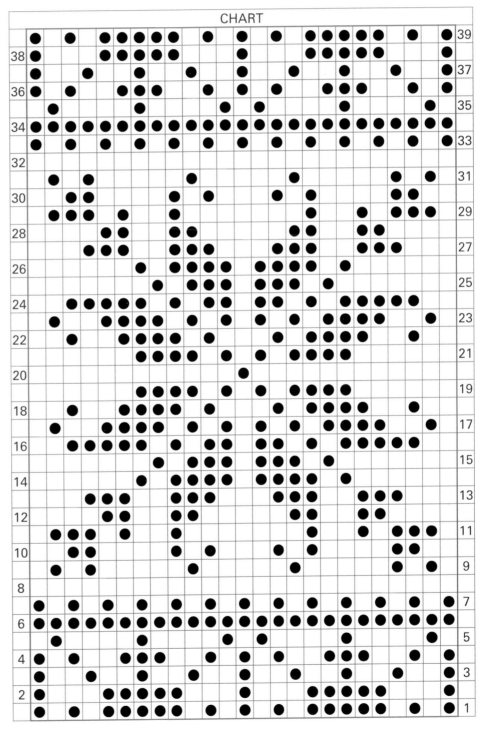

CHART

KEY ● COLOUR A
☐ COLOUR B

These 2 rows form **rib**.
Using B, work 11 rows more in rib.
**14th row.** P10, p2tog, (p7, p2tog) 14 times, p10. 133 sts.
Change to 4 mm needles and work as follows:-
** **1st row.** K2B, * work the next 25 sts as given for 1st row of chart from right to left, k1B, rep from * to last st, k1B.
**2nd row.** P1B, * p1B, work the next 25 sts as given for 2nd row of chart from left to right, rep from * to last 2 sts, p2B.
1st and 2nd rows set position of chart.
Beg with 3rd row of chart work 37 rows. **
Using B only work as follows:-
**Next row.** (P13, p2tog) 8 times, p13. 125 sts.
**1st row.** Knit.
**2nd row.** Purl.
Last 2 rows form **st-st** (stocking stitch).
Cont in st-st until blanket measures 26 cm, 10¼ in, ending with a rs row.
**Next row.** P10, m1, (p15, m1) 7 times, p10. 133 sts.
Work from ** to ** once.
Using B only work as follows:-
**Next row.** (P13, p2tog) 8 times, p13. 125 sts.
Cont in st-st until blanket

measures 48 cm, 19 in, ending with a rs row.
**Next row.** P10, m1, (p15, m1) 7 times, p10. 133 sts.
Work from ** to ** once.
**Next row.** Using B only, p10, m1, (p8, m1) 14 times, p11. 148 sts.
Change to 3¼ mm needles and using B, work 12 rows in rib.
Using A, work 2 rows more.
Cast off in rib.

## SIDE BORDERS (Both alike)

With rs facing, using 3¼ mm needles and B, pick up and knit 12 sts evenly along rib, 170 sts evenly along side edge and 12 sts evenly along rib. 194 sts.
**1st row.** * P2, k2, rep from * to last 2 sts, p2.

**2nd row.** K2, * p2, k2, rep from * to end.
These 2 rows form **rib**.
Work 10 rows more in rib.
Using A, work 2 rows more in rib. Cast off in rib.

## TO COMPLETE

Pin out blanket to the measurement given. Cover with clean, damp tea towels and leave until dry. See ball band for washing and further care instructions.

~~~~~~~~~~

*Little Holiday Blanket*
## TENSION
22 sts and 30 rows to 10 cm, 4 in, over pattern 1 and 3, 21 sts

and 34 rows to 10 cm, 4 in, over pattern 2 on 4 mm needles, or the size required to give correct tension.

Using 3¼ mm needles, colour A and thumb method cast on 125 sts.
**1st row.** Knit.
This row is called **g-st** (garter stitch).
Work 9 rows more in g-st.
Change to 4 mm needles and work as follows:-
**1st row.** Knit.
**2nd row.** * K1, p3, rep from * to last st, k1.
1st and 2nd rows form **patt 1**.
Cont in patt 1 until blanket measures 26 cm, 10¼ in, ending with a rs row.
**Next row.** P11, p2tog, (p23, p2tog) 4 times, p12. 120 sts.
Work as follows:-
**1st row.** Knit.

**2nd row.** Purl.
**3rd row.** Knit.
**4th row.** Knit.
From 1st to 4th row forms **patt 2**.
Cont in patt 2 until blanket measures approximately 50 cm, 19¾ in, ending with 3rd row of patt.
**Next row.** P12, m1, (p24, m1) 4 times, p12. 125 sts.
Work as follows:-
**1st row.** K1, * p1, k1, rep from * to end.
**2nd row.** * P1, k1, rep from * to last st, p1.
**3rd row.** Knit.
**4th row.** Purl.
**5th row.** P1, * k1, p1, rep from * to end.
**6th row.** K1, * p1, k1, rep from * to end.
**7th row.** Knit.
**8th row.** Purl.
From 1st to 8th row forms

**patt 3**.
Cont in patt 3 until blanket measures approximately 73 cm, 28¾ in, ending with 2nd row of patt.
Change to 3¼ mm needles and work 9 rows in g-st.
Cast off knitways.

## SIDE BORDERS (Both alike)
With rs facing, using 3¼ mm needles pick up and knit 8 sts evenly along rib, 154 sts evenly along side edge and 8 sts evenly along rib. 170 sts.
Work 8 rows in g-st.
Cast off knitways.

## TO COMPLETE
Pin out blanket to the measurement given. Cover with clean, damp tea towels and leave until dry. See ball band for washing and further care instructions.

# Little Crocus Dress & Rosehip Tunic

## MEASUREMENTS

| Ages | | | | | |
|---|---|---|---|---|---|
| Mths | 6-12 | 1-2 years | 2-3 years | 4-5 years | 6-7 years |
| **To Fit Chest** | | | | | |
| cm | 46 | 51 | 56 | 61 | 66 |
| in | 18 | 20 | 22 | 24 | 26 |
| **Actual Measurement** | | | | | |
| cm | 47 | 53 | 58 | 64 | 67 |
| in | 18½ | 21 | 22¾ | 25¼ | 26½ |
| **Full Length** | | | | | |
| cm | 34 | 37 | 44 | 53 | 58 |
| in | 13½ | 14½ | 17¼ | 21 | 22¾ |
| **Short Sleeve Length (approximately)** | | | | | |
| cm | 3 | 4 | 4 | 5 | 5 |
| in | 1¼ | 1½ | 1½ | 2 | 2 |

## MATERIALS
**Little Crocus Dress** Bamboo Cotton DK

| | | | | | | |
|---|---|---|---|---|---|---|
| M 625 Old Gold | 100g balls | 2M | 2M | 2M | 3M | 3M |
| C 530 White | | 1C | 1C | 1C | 1C | 1C |

**Rosehip Tunic** Merino Blend DK

| | | | | | | |
|---|---|---|---|---|---|---|
| Shade 703 Cranberry | 50g balls | 3 | 3 | 4 | 6 | 6 |

Also suitable for any King Cole DK yarns.
It is essential to work to the stated tension to achieve the correct size of garment.

## Needles
1 pair 3¼ mm (UK 10 – USA 3) knitting needles
1 pair 4 mm (UK 8 – USA 6) knitting needles
Cable needle
Stitch holders
6[6:7:7:7] buttons

## Tension
22 sts and 28 rows to 10 cm, 4 in, over stocking stitch on 4 mm needles or the size required to give the correct tension.

# Little Crocus Dress

## FRONT
Using 3¼ mm needles, C and thumb method cast on 76[84:92:102:108] sts.
**1st row.** Knit.
This row is called **g-st** (garter stitch).
Work 1 row more in g-st.
Change to 4 mm needles and M.

**1st row.** K20[24:28:33:36], (p3, k8) 3 times, p3, k20[24:28:33:36].
**2nd row.** P20[24:28:33:36], (k3, p8) 3 times, k3, p20[24:28:33:36].
These 2 rows form **patt**.
Cont in patt, shaping side seams by dec 1 st at each

end of 11th[5th:9th:7th:7th] and 3[4:5:7:8] foll 12th rows.
68[74:80:86:90] sts.
Work 4 rows, ending with a **rs** row. (Front should measure approximately 19.5[21.5:27.5:35.5:39.5] cm, 7¾[8½:10¾:14:15½] in).
**Next row.** P16[19:22:25:27],

(k1, k2tog, p2, p2tog, p2togtbl, p2) 3 times, k1, k2tog, p16[19:22:25:27]. 58[64:70:76:80] sts.
Now work in cable patt as follows:
**1st row.** K16[19:22:25:27], (p2, C6B) 3 times, p2, k16[19:22:25:27].

**2nd row.** P16[19:22:25:27], (k2, p6) 3 times, k2, p16[19:22:25:27].
**3rd row.** K16[19:22:25:27], (p2, k6) 3 times, p2, k16[19:22:25:27].
**4th row.** P16[19:22:25:27], (k2, p6) 3 times, k2, p16[19:22:25:27].
**5th and 6th rows.** As 3rd and 4th rows.
These 6 rows form **cable patt.**
Keeping cable patt correct throughout, cont as follows:
**Shape Armholes**
Cast off 3 sts at beg of next 2 rows. 52[58:64:70:74] sts.
Dec 1 st at each end of next and foll 2[2:3:3:3] alt rows. 46[52:56:62:66] sts.
Work 7[9:9:11:13] rows, ending with a ws row.
**Shape Front Neck**
**Next row.** Patt 17[19:22:23:25] sts and turn, leaving rem 29[33:34:39:41] sts on a holder.
Working on these 17[19:22:23:25] sts only proceed as follows:-
Keeping patt correct, dec 1 st at neck edge of next 4 rows,

then on foll 2[2:3:3:3] alt rows, then on 2 foll 4th rows. 9[11:13:14:16] sts.
Work 3 rows, ending with a ws row. (Armhole should measure approximately 12[13:14:15:16] cm, 4¾[5¼:5½:6:6¼] in).
**Shape Shoulder**
Cast off 4[5:6:7:8] sts at beg of next row.
Work 1 row.
Cast off rem 5[6:7:7:8] sts.
Return to sts left on holder and slip centre 12[14:12:16:16] sts onto another holder (for Neckband), patt to end. 17[19:22:23:25] sts.
Keeping patt correct, dec 1 st at neck edge of next 4 rows, then on foll 2[2:3:3:3] alt rows, then on 2 foll 4th rows. 9[11:13:14:16] sts.
Work 4 rows, ending with a **rs** row.
**Shape Shoulder**
Cast off 4[5:6:7:8] sts at beg of next row.
Work 1 row.
Cast off rem 5[6:7:7:8] sts.

**RIGHT BACK**
Using 3¼ mm needles, C and thumb method cast on 41[45:49:54:57] sts.
Work in g-st for 2 rows as given for Front, ending with a ws row.
Change to 4 mm needles and M.
**1st row.** Knit to last 5 sts, (p1, k1) twice, p1.
**2nd row.** P1, (k1, p1) twice, purl to end.
**3rd row.** Knit to last 5 sts, (k1, p1) twice, k1.
**4th row.** K1, (p1, k1) twice, purl to end.
These 4 rows set the sts – back opening edge 5 sts in Irish moss st with all other sts in st-st.
Cont as now set, shaping side seam by dec 1 st at beg of 9th[3rd:7th:5th:5th] and 3[4:5:7:8] foll 12th rows. 37[40:43:46:48] sts.
Work 4 rows, ending with a **rs** row.

**Next row.** Patt 5 sts, p1[2:0:2:3], p2tog, (p2[2:3:3:3], p2tog) 7 times, p1[3:1:2:3]. 29[32:35:38:40] sts.
Still working back opening edge 5 sts in Irish moss st and all other sts in st-st, cont as follows:
Work 6 rows, ending with a ws row.
**Shape Armhole**
Cast off 3 sts at beg of next row. 26[29:32:35:37] sts.
Work 1 row.
Dec 1 st at armhole edge of next and foll 2[2:3:3:3] alt rows. 23[26:28:31:33] sts.
Work 27[29:31:33:35] rows, ending with a ws row.
**Shape Shoulder**
Cast off 4[5:6:7:8] sts at beg of next row, then 5[6:7:7:8] sts at beg of foll alt row.
Work 1 row, ending with a ws row.
Break yarn and leave rem 14[15:15:17:17] sts on a holder (for Neckband).
Mark positions for 6[6:7:7:7] buttons along right back opening edge – first to come in 29th row up from cast-on edge, last to come just below sts left on holder, and rem 4[4:5:5:5] buttons evenly spaced between.

**LEFT BACK**
Using 3¼ mm needles, C and thumb method cast on 41[45:49:54:57] sts.
Work in g-st for 2 rows as given for Front, ending with a ws row.
Change to 4 mm needles and M.
**1st row.** P1, (k1, p1) twice, knit to end.
**2nd row.** Purl to last 5 sts, (p1, k1) twice, p1.
**3rd row.** K1, (p1, k1) twice, knit to end.
**4th row.** Purl to last 5 sts, (k1, p1) twice, k1.
These 4 rows set the sts – back opening edge 5 sts in Irish moss st with all other sts in st-st.
Cont as now set, shaping side seam by dec 1 st at end of

9th[3rd:7th:5th:5th] and foll 12th row. 39[43:47:52:55] sts.
Work 1[7:3:5:5] rows, ending with a ws row.
**Next row.** Patt 1 st, work 2 tog, yrn (to make a buttonhole), patt to end.
Working a further 5[5:6:6:6] buttonholes in this way to correspond with positions marked for buttons on Right Back and noting that no further reference will be made to buttonholes, cont as follows:
Dec 1 st at end of 10th[4th:8th:6th:6th] and 1[2:3:5:6] foll 12th rows. 37[40:43:46:48] sts.
Work 4 rows, ending with a **rs** row.
**Next row.** P1[3:1:2:3], p2tog, (p2[2:3:3:3], p2tog) 7 times, p1[2:0:2:3], patt 5 sts. 29[32:35:38:40] sts.
Still working back opening edge 5 sts in Irish moss st and all other sts in st-st, cont as follows:
Work 7 rows, ending with a **rs** row.
**Shape Armhole**
Cast off 3 sts at beg of next row. 26[29:32:35:37] sts.
Dec 1 st at armhole edge of next and foll 2[2:3:3:3] alt rows. 23[26:28:31:33] sts.
Work 28[30:32:34:36] rows, ending with a **rs** row.
**Shape Shoulder**
Cast off 4[5:6:7:8] sts at beg of next row, then 5[6:7:7:8] sts at beg of foll alt row, ending with a ws row.
Break yarn and leave rem 14[15:15:17:17] sts on a holder (for Neckband).

**SLEEVES (Both alike)**
Using 3¼ mm needles, C and thumb method, cast on 46[50:54:60:64] sts.
Work 2 rows in g- st as given for Front.
Change to 4 mm needles and M.
**1st row.** Inc in first st, knit to last st, inc in last st. 48[52:56:62:66] sts.
**2nd row.** Purl.
These 2 rows are called **st-st** (stocking stitch) **and start of sleeve shaping.**
Cont in st-st (throughout) inc 1 st at each end of 1st[1st:1st:3rd:3rd] and foll alt[4th:4th:4th:4th] row. 52[56:60:66:70] sts.
Work 1[3:3:3:3] rows, ending with a ws row.
**Shape Top**
Cast off 4[3:4:3:3] sts at beg of next 6[2:10:4:10] rows, then 5[4:0:4:4] sts at beg of foll 2[8:0:8:4] rows.
Cast off rem 18[18:20:22:24] sts.

**NECKBAND**
Join shoulder seams.
With rs facing, using 3¼ mm needles and C, knit across 14[15:15:17:17] sts on left back holder, pick up and knit 20[20:22:22:22] sts down left side of neck, knit across 12[14:12:16:16] sts on front holder as follows: (k2togtbl) 0[0:0:1:1] times, k4[5:4:4:4], k2tog, k2togtbl, k4[5:4:4:4], (k2tog) 0[0:0:1:1] times. pick up and knit 20[20:22:22:22] sts up right side of neck, then knit across 14[15:15:17:17] sts on right back holder. 78[82:84:90:90] sts.
Work in g-st for 2 rows as given for Front, ending with a **rs** row.
Cast off knitways.

**TO MAKE UP**
Fold sleeves in half lengthways and placing folds to shoulder seams sew sleeves in position. Join side and sleeve seams. Sew on buttons.
Pin out dress to the measurements given. Cover with clean, damp tea towels and leave to dry. See ball band for washing and further care instructions.

## Rosehip Tunic

**FRONT**
Work as given for Front of Little Crocus Dress using one colour only.

**RIGHT BACK**
Work as given for Right Back of Little Crocus Dress using one colour only.

**LEFT BACK**
Work as given for Left Back of Little Crocus Dress using one colour only.

**NECKBAND**
Work as given for Neckband of Little Crocus Dress using one colour only.

**ARMHOLE BORDERS (Both alike)**
With rs facing, using 3¼ mm needles, pick up and knit 58[62:66:72:76] sts evenly all round armhole edge.
Work in g-st for 2 rows as given for Front, ending with a **rs** row.
Cast off knitways.

**TO MAKE UP**
Join side and armhole border seams. Sew on buttons.
Pin out tunic to the measurements given. Cover with clean, damp tea towels and leave to dry. See ball band for washing and further care instructions.

# Little Folk Cardie & Sunny Little Cardie

## MEASUREMENTS

### Ages

| Mths | 0-9 | 9-18 | 18-24 | 3-4 years | 5-7 years |
|---|---|---|---|---|---|
| **To Fit Chest** | | | | | |
| cm | 41-46 | 46-51 | 51-56 | 56-61 | 61-66 |
| in | 16-18 | 18-20 | 20-22 | 22-24 | 24-26 |
| **Actual Measurement (excluding the vent)** | | | | | |
| cm | 50 | 55 | 60 | 65 | 70 |
| in | 19¾ | 21¾ | 23¾ | 25½ | 27½ |
| **Full Length** | | | | | |
| cm | 22 | 26 | 31 | 35 | 41 |
| in | 8¾ | 10¼ | 12 | 13¾ | 16 |
| **Sleeve Length** | | | | | |
| cm | 17 | 20 | 24 | 29 | 33 |
| in | 6½ | 8 | 9½ | 11½ | 13 |
| **Short** | | | | | |
| cm | 4 | 5 | 5 | 6 | 6 |
| in | 1½ | 2 | 2 | 2½ | 2½ |

## MATERIALS

**Little Folk Cardie**  Merino Blend DK

| shade 41 Oatmeal | 50g balls | 2 | 4 | 5 | 6 | 7 |
|---|---|---|---|---|---|---|

**Sunny Little Cardie**  Bamboo Cotton DK

| shade 634 Crimson | 100g balls | 1 | 2 | 2 | 2 | 3 |
|---|---|---|---|---|---|---|

Also suitable for any King Cole DK yarns.
It is essential to work to the stated tension to achieve the correct size of garment.

### Needles
1 pair 4 mm (UK 8 – USA 6) knitting needles
1 pair 3¼ mm (UK 10 – USA 3) knitting needles
3 buttons

### Tension
22 sts and 30 rows to 10 cm, 4 in, over Irish moss stitch on 4 mm needles or the size required to give the correct tension.

## BACK

Using 4 mm needles and thumb method cast on 73[81:89:95:103] sts.

**1st row. (rs)** (K1, p1) 13[15:16:17:19] times, k21[21:25:27:27], (p1, k1) 13[15:16:17:19] times.

**2nd row.** (P1, k1) 13[15:16:17:19] times, p1[0:1:1:0], k19[21:23:25:27], p1[0:1:1:0], (k1, p1) 13[15:16:17:19] times.

**3rd row.** As 2nd row.

**4th row.** (K1, p1) 13[15:16:17:19] times, k21[21:25:27:27], (p1, k1) 13[15:16:17:19] times.

**5th row.** (K1, p1) 13[15:16:17:19] times, k1[0:1:1:0], p19[21:23:25:27], k1[0:1:1:0], (p1, k1) 13[15:16:17:19] times.

**6th row.** (P1, k1) 13[15:16:17:19] times, p1[0:1:1:0], k19[21:23:25:27], p1[0:1:1:0], (k1, p1) 13[15:16:17:19] times.

**7th row.** (P1, k1) 13[15:16:17:19] times, p21[21:25:27:27], (k1, p1) 13[15:16:17:19] times.

**8th row.** (K1, p1) 13[15:16:17:19] times, k21[21:25:27:27], (p1, k1) 13[15:16:17:19] times.

From 5th to 8th row forms **Irish moss-st and centre panel.**

Work as follows:-

**1st row.** Patt 27[30:33:35:38] sts, p2tog, p15[17:19:21:23], p2togtbl, patt 27[30:33:35:38] sts. 71[79:87:93:101] sts.

**2nd row.** Patt 27[30:33:35:38] sts, k17[19:21:23:25], patt 27[30:33:35:38] sts.

1st and 2nd rows form centre panel shaping.

Work 22[32:16:4:68] rows dec 1 st at each side of centre panel as before in 5th[5th:5th:0:7th] and every foll 6th[6th:6th:0:8th] row. 65[69:83:93:85] sts.

### For 3rd and 4th sizes only

Work [28:48] rows dec 1 st at each side of centre panel as before in next and every foll 8th row. [75:81] sts.

### For all sizes
### Shape Armholes

Work 4[4:5:5:5] rows dec 1 st at each end of every row **AT THE SAME TIME** dec 1 st at each side of centre panel as before on 1st[0:5th:1st:5th] row. 55[61:63:69:73] sts.

Work 16[18:17:21:21] rows dec 1 st at each side of centre panel only as before in 3rd[1st:8th:4th:10th] and every foll 6th[8th:8th:8th:10th] row. 49[55:59:63:69] sts.

Work 6[6:6:6:8] rows without shaping.

**Next row.** Patt 23[26:28:30:33] sts, p3tog, patt 23[26:28:30:33] sts. 47[53:57:61:67] sts.

**Next row.** Patt.

Cont in Irish moss-st until armhole measures 11[12:13:14:15] cm, 4¼[4¾:5¼:5½:6] in, ending with a ws row.

### Shape Shoulders

Cast off 6[7:8:8:9] sts in patt at beg of next 2 rows. 35[39:41:45:49] sts.

Cast off 6[7:8:8:10] sts in patt at beg of next 2 rows. 23[25:25:29:29] sts.

Cast off rem 23[25:25:29:29] sts.

## LEFT FRONT

Using 4 mm needles and thumb method cast on 30[33:36:38:41] sts.

Work as follows:-

**1st row. (rs)** * K1, p1, rep from * to last 0[1:0:0:1] sts, k0[1:0:0:1].

**2nd row.** P0[1:0:0:1], * k1, p1, rep from * to end.

**3rd row.** * P1, k1, rep from * to last 0[1:0:0:1] sts, p0[1:0:0:1].

**4th row.** K0[1:0:0:1], * p1, k1, rep from * to end.

From 1st to 4th row forms **Irish moss-st.**

Work 28[38:50:58:74] rows in Irish moss-st.

**Shape Armhole**

**1st row.** Patt2tog (armhole edge), patt to end. 29[32:35:37:40] sts.

**2nd row.** Patt to last 2 sts, patt2tog. 28[31:34:36:39] sts.

1st and 2nd rows set armhole shapings.

Work 2[2:3:3:3] rows dec 1 st at armhole edge in every row. 26[29:31:33:36] sts.

Cont without shaping until armhole measures 3.5[4.5:4.5:5.5:6.5] cm, 1¼[1¾:1¾:2¼:2½] in, ending with a rs row.

**Shape Neck**

**Next row.** Cast off 6[7:7:9:9]sts in patt, patt to end. 20[22:24:24:27] sts.

Work 4 rows dec 1 st at neck edge in every row. 16[18:20:20:23] sts.

Work 7 rows dec 1 st at neck edge in next and every foll alt row. 12[14:16:16:19] sts.

Cont without shaping until armhole measures 11[12:13:14:15] cm, 4¼[4¾:5¼:5½:6] in, ending with a ws row.

**Shape Shoulder**

**Next row.** Cast off 6[7:8:8:9] sts in patt, patt to end. 6[7:8:8:10] sts.

**Next row.** Patt.

Cast off rem 6[7:8:8:10] sts in patt.

## RIGHT FRONT

Using 4 mm needles and thumb method cast on 30[33:36:38:41] sts.

Work as follows:-

**1st row. (rs)** K0[1:0:0:1], * p1, k1, rep from * to end.

**2nd row.** * P1, k1, rep from * to last 0[1:0:0:1] sts, p0[1:0:0:1].

**3rd row.** P0[1:0:0:1], * k1, p1, rep from * to end.

**4th row.** * K1, p1, rep from * to last 0[1:0:0:1] sts, k0[1:0:0:1].

From 1st to 4th row forms **Irish moss-st.**

Work 28[38:50:58:74] rows in Irish moss-st.

**Shape Armhole**

**1st row.** Patt to last 2 sts, patt2tog (armhole edge). 29[32:35:37:40] sts.

**2nd row.** Patt2tog, patt to end. 28[31:34:36:39] sts.

1st and 2nd rows set armhole shapings.

Work 2[2:3:3:3] rows dec 1 st at armhole edge in every row. 26[29:31:33:36] sts.

Cont without shaping until armhole measures 3.5[4.5:4.5:5.5:6.5] cm, 1¼[1¾:1¾:2¼:2½] in, ending with a ws row.

**Shape Neck**

**Next row.** Cast off 6[7:7:9:9] sts in patt, patt to end. 20[22:24:24:27] sts.

**Next row.** Patt.

Work 4 rows dec 1 st at neck edge in every row. 16[18:20:20:23] sts.

Work 7 rows dec 1 st at neck edge in next and every foll alt row. 12[14:16:16:19] sts.

Cont without shaping until armhole measures 11[12:13:14:15] cm, 4¼[4¾:5¼:5½:6] in, ending with a rs row.

**Shape Shoulder**

**Next row.** Cast off 6[7:8:8:9] sts in patt, patt to end. 6[7:8:8:10] sts.

**Next row.** Patt.

Cast off rem 6[7:8:8:10] sts in patt.

## LONG SLEEVES (Both alike)

Using 4 mm needles and thumb method cast on 31[33:33:37:39] sts.

Work as follows:-

**1st row. (rs)** * K1, p1, rep from * to last st, k1.

**2nd row.** P1, * k1, p1, rep from * to end.

**3rd row.** * P1, k1, rep from * to last st, p1.

**4th row.** K1, * p1, k1, rep from * to end.

From 1st to 4th row forms **Irish moss-st.**

Cont in Irish moss-st inc 1 st at each end of next and every foll 6th[6th:6th:8th:8th] row to 45[45:49:57:57] sts, working inc sts in Irish moss-st.

**For 2nd, 3rd and 5th sizes only**

Inc 1 st at each end of every foll [8th:8th:10th] row to [49:53:61] sts, working inc sts in Irish moss-st.

**For all sizes**

Cont without shaping until sleeve measures 17[20:24:29:33] cm, 6½[8:9½:11½:13] in, ending with a ws row.

**Shape Sleeve Top**

Work 4 [4:5:5:5] rows dec 1 st at each end of every row.

37[41:43:47:51] sts.
Work 0[0:1:1:1] rows more without shaping.
Cast off 3[4:3:3:2] sts in patt at beg of next 4[4:6:2:6] rows.
25[25:25:41:39] sts.
Cast off 4[4:4:4:3] sts in patt at beg of next 4[4:4:8:10] rows. 9 sts.
Cast off rem 9 sts in patt.

## SHORT SLEEVES (Both alike)
Using 4 mm needles and thumb method cast on 41[45:49:53:57] sts.
Working in Irish moss-st as given for Long Sleeves inc 1 st at each end of 3rd and foll 3rd[5th:5th:7th:7th] row to 45[49:53:57:61] sts, working inc sts in Irish moss-st.
Cont without shaping until sleeve measures 4[5:5:6:6] cm, 1½[2:2:2½:2½] in, ending with a ws row.

### Shape Sleeve Top
Work as given for Shape Sleeve Top of Long Sleeves.

## NECKBAND
Join shoulder seams. With rs facing, using 3¼ mm needles pick up and knit 26[27:31:33:33] sts evenly along right side of neck, 23[25:25:29:29] sts from cast off sts at back of neck and 26[27:31:33:33] sts evenly along left side of neck.

75[79:87:95:95] sts.
Cast off knitways.

## TO MAKE UP
Fold sleeves in half lengthways, then placing sleeve top folds to shoulder seams, sew sleeves in position. Join side and sleeve seams. Make three button loops and attach to the left front for a boy and the right front for a girl as illustrated. Sew on buttons. Pin out cardie to the measurement given. Cover with clean, damp tea towels and leave until dry. See ball band for washing and further care instructions.

# Willow Coat & Little Mandarin Coat

## MEASUREMENTS

### Ages

| Mths | 0-9 | 9-18 | 18-24 | 3-5 years | 5-7 years |
|---|---|---|---|---|---|
| **To Fit Chest** | | | | | |
| cm | 41-46 | 46-51 | 51-56 | 56-61 | 61-66 |
| in | 16-18 | 18-20 | 20-22 | 22-24 | 24-26 |
| **Actual Measurement** | | | | | |
| cm | 50 | 55 | 60 | 66 | 71 |
| in | 19¾ | 21¾ | 23¾ | 26 | 28 |
| **Full Length** | | | | | |
| cm | 28 | 32 | 38 | 42 | 48 |
| in | 11 | 12½ | 15 | 16½ | 19 |
| **Sleeve Length** | | | | | |
| cm | 17 | 20 | 24 | 29 | 33 |
| in | 6½ | 8 | 9½ | 11½ | 13 |

## MATERIALS

**Willow Coat** Merino Blend DK

| shade 854 Fern | 50g balls | 4 | 5 | 6 | 8 | 10 |
|---|---|---|---|---|---|---|

**Little Mandarin Coat** Bamboo Cotton DK

| shade 628 Mauve | 100g balls | 2 | 2 | 3 | 4 | 4 |
|---|---|---|---|---|---|---|

Also suitable for any King Cole DK yarns.
It is essential to work to the stated tension to achieve the correct size of garment.

**Needles**
1 pair 3¼ mm (UK 10 - USA 3) knitting needles
1 pair 4 mm (UK 8 - USA 6) knitting needles
8 Buttons

**Tension**
22 sts and 28 rows to 10cm, 4in, over stocking stitch and 22 sts and 36 rows to 10cm, 4in, over moss-stitch on 4mm needles or the size required to give the correct tension.

# Willow Coat

## BACK
Using 3¼ mm needles and thumb method cast on 89[99:107:117:127] sts.
**1st row.** K35[39:42:46:50], (k1, p1) 9[10:11:12:13] times, k1, k35[39:42:46:50].
Rep 1st row 3 times.
Change to 4 mm needles and work as follows:-
**1st row.** K35[39:42:46:50], (k1, p1) 9[10:11:12:13] times, k1, k35[39:42:46:50].
**2nd row.** P35[39:42:46:50], (k1, p1) 9[10:11:12:13] times, k1, p35[39:42:46:50].
These 2 rows form **patt (st-st with moss-st vent).**
Work 2[2:2:2:6] rows as set.
**Next row.** K2tog, k33[37:40:44:48], k2tog, moss stitch 15[17:19:21:23] sts, k2tog, 85[95:103:113:123] sts.
**Last row sets side and vent decs.**
**Remember that the moss stitch vent stitches will decrease by 2 sts each time a decrease row is worked and the stocking stitch at the side will decrease by 1 st.**
Work 1[1:5:5:5] rows without shaping.
**For 1st and 2nd sizes only**
Work 4[2] rows dec 4 sts **as before** in next and every foll alt[0] row. 77[91] sts.
**For 3rd, 4th and 5th sizes only**
Work [12:54:60] rows dec 4 sts **as before** in next and every foll

6th row. [95:77:83] sts.
**For all sizes**
Work 22[30:30:6:6] rows dec 4
sts **as before** in next and every
foll 4th row. 53[59:63:69:75] sts.
**Next row.** K22[25:27:30:33], C9F,
knit to end.
**Next row.** * P1, k1, rep from * to
last st, p1.
Last row forms **moss-st.**
Cont in moss-st (throughout)
until back measures
17[19:25:33:37] cm,
6½[7½:9¾:13:14½] in, ending
with a ws row.
**Shape Armholes**
Work 3[4:4:5:5] rows dec 1
st at each end of every row.
47[51:55:59:65] sts.
Cont without shaping
until armholes measure
12[13:14:15:16] cm,
4¾[5¼:5½:6:6¼] in, ending with
a ws row.
**Shape Shoulders**
Cast off 7[7:8:8:9] sts in moss-
st at beg of next 2 rows.
33[37:39:43:47] sts.
Cast off 7[7:8:8:10] sts in
moss-st at beg of next 2 rows.
19[23:23:27:27] sts.
Cast off rem 19[23:23:27:27] sts
in moss-st.

## LEFT FRONT
Using 3¼ mm needles and
thumb method cast on
44[48:52:58:62] sts.

**1st row.** Knit to last 4 sts,
(p1, k1) twice.
**2nd row.** S1, k1, p1, knit to end.
Rep last 2 rows once.
Change to 4 mm needles and
work as follows:-
**1st row.** Knit to last 4 sts,
(p1, k1) twice.
**2nd row.** S1, k1, p1, k1, purl to
end.
These 2 rows form **patt.**
Work 2[2:2:2:6] rows as set.
**For 1st and 2nd sizes only**
Work 6[4] rows dec 1 st at side
edge (beg) in next and every foll
alt row. 41[46] sts.
**For 3rd, 4th and 5th sizes only**
Work [18:60:66] rows dec 1 st
at side edge (beg) in next and
every foll 6th row. [49:48:51] sts.
**For all sizes**
Work 23[31:31:7:7] rows dec 1
st at side edge in next and every
foll 4th row. 35[38:41:46:49] sts.
**Next row.** S1, k1[0:1:0:1], * p1,
k1, rep from * to last st, p1.
**Next row.** P1, * k1,p1, rep from *
to last 0[1:0:1:0] sts, k0[1:0:1:0]
sts.
Last 2 rows form **moss-st.**
Cont in moss-st (throughout)
until left front measures
17[19:25:33:37] cm,
6½[7½:9¾:13:14½] in, ending
with a ws row.
**Shape Armhole**
Work 3[4:4:5:5] rows dec 1 st at
armhole edge (beg of next row)
in every row. 32[34:37:41:44]
sts.
Cont without shaping until
armhole measures
8[9:9:10:11] cm, 3[3½:3½:4:4¼]
in, ending with a rs row.
**Shape Neck**
**Next row.** Cast off
13[15:15:19:19] sts in patt, patt
to end. 19[19:22:22:25] sts.
Work 2 rows dec 1 st at
neck edge in every row.
17[17:20:20:23] sts.
Work 2 rows dec 1 st at neck
edge in 1st row. 16[16:19:19:22]
sts.
Work 5 [5:9:9:9] rows dec 1 st at

neck edge in next and every foll
4th row. 14[14:16:16:19] sts.
Cont without shaping
until armhole measures
12[13:14:15:16] cm,
4¾[5¼:5½:6:6¼] in, ending with
a ws row.
**Shape Shoulder**
**Next row.** Cast off 7[7:8:8:9] sts
in patt, patt to end. 7[7:8:8:10]
sts.
**Next row.** Patt.
Cast off rem 7[7:8:8:10] sts in
patt.
Mark positions for 3 pairs of
buttons – first pair to be 1.5 cm,
½ in, up from beg of moss st,
third pair to be 1.5 cm, ½ in,
down from neck and second pair
halfway between.

## RIGHT FRONT
Using 3¼ mm needles and
thumb method cast on
44[48:52:58:62] sts.
**1st row.** S1, p1, k1, p1, knit to
end.
**2nd row.** Knit to last 3 sts, p1,
k1, p1.
Rep last 2 rows once.
Change to 4 mm needles and
work as follows:-
**1st row.** S1, p1, k1, p1, knit to
end.
**2nd row.** Purl to last 4 sts, (k1,
p1) twice .
These 2 rows form **patt.**
Work 2[2:2:2:6] rows as set.
**For 1st and 2nd sizes only**
Work 6[4] rows dec 1 st at side
edge (end) in next and every foll
alt row. 41[46] sts.
**For 3rd, 4th and 5th sizes only**
Work [18:60:66] rows dec 1 st
at side edge (end) in next and
every foll 6th row. [49:48:51] sts.
**For all sizes**
Work 23[31:31:7:7] rows dec 1
st at side edge in next and every
foll 4th row. 35[38:41:46:49] sts.
**Next row.** P1, * k1, p1, rep
from * to last 0[1:0:1:0] sts,
k0[1:0:1:0].
**Next row.** S1, p0[1:0:1:0], * k1,
p1, rep from * to end.

Last 2 rows form **moss-st**.
Cont in moss-st (throughout) remembering to work 3 sets of buttonholes to correspond to markers as follows:-
**Buttonhole row.** Patt 3, yrn, patt2 tog, patt 8[10:12:13:13], yrn, patt2 tog, patt to end.
Cont until right front measures 17[19:25:33:37]cm, 6½[7½:9¾:13:14½] in, ending with a ws row.
**Shape Armhole**
Work 3[4:4:5:5] rows dec 1 st at armhole edge (end of next row) in every row. 32[34:37:41:44] sts.
Cont without shaping until armhole measures 8[9:9:10:11] cm, 3[3½:3½:4:4¼] in, ending with a ws row.
**Shape Neck**
**Next row.** Cast off 13[15:15:19:19] sts in patt, patt to end. 19[19:22:22:25] sts.
**Next row.** Patt.
Work 2 rows dec 1 st at neck edge in every row. 17[17:20:20:23] sts.
Work 2 rows dec 1 st at neck edge in 1st row. 16[16:19:19:22] sts.
Work 5 [5:9:9:9] rows dec 1 st at neck edge in next and every foll 4th row. 14[14:16:16:19] sts.
Cont without shaping until armhole measures 12[13:14:15:16] cm, 4¾[5¼:5½:6:6¼] in, ending with a rs row.
**Shape Shoulder**
**Next row.** Cast off 7[7:8:8:9] sts in patt, patt to end. 7[7:8:8:10] sts.
**Next row.** Patt.
Cast off rem 7[7:8:8:10] sts in patt.

**SLEEVES (Both alike)**
Using 3¼ mm needles and thumb method cast on 31[33:33:37:39] sts.
**1st row.** Knit.
This row is called **g-st** (garter stitch).

Work 3 rows more in g-st.
Change to 4 mm needles and work in st-st (throughout) inc 1 st at each end of 5th and every foll 4th[4th:4th:6th:6th] row to 39[39:41:49:47] sts.
Inc 1 st at each end of every foll 6th[6th:6th:8th:8th] row to 45[49:53:57:61] sts.
Cont without shaping until sleeve measures 17[20:24:29:33] cm, 6½[8:9½11½:13] in, ending with a ws row.
**Shape Top**
Work 3[4:4:5:5] rows dec 1 st at each end of every row. 39[41:45:47:51] sts.
Work 1[0:0:1:1] rows without shaping.
Cast off 7[4:4:4:5] sts at beg of next 2[8:4:2:6] rows. 25[9:29:39:21] sts.
**For 1st, 3rd, 4th and 5th sizes only**
Cast off 8[5:5:6] sts at beg of next 2[4:6:2] rows. 9 sts.
**For all sizes**
Cast off rem 9 sts.

**COLLAR**
Join shoulder seams.
Place a marker on the cast off sts of the Front Neck mid way between top buttonholes and a 2nd marker on the Left front mid way between top button markers.
With rs facing, using 3¼ mm needles and starting 1 cm to the left of the 1st marker (to allow for the collar edging), pick up and knit 16[16:21:21:21] sts evenly up right side of neck, 19[23:23:27:27] sts from back of neck and 16[16:21:21:21] sts evenly down left side of neck, ending 1 cm to right of 2nd marker. 51[55:65:69:69] sts.
Work 2 rows in st-st.
Change to 4 mm needles.
Work 2 rows in st-st.
**Next row.** K1, (inc in next st) 10[12:12:14:14] times, knit to last 11[13:13:15:15] sts, (inc in next

st) 10[12:12:14:14] times, k1. 71[79:89:97:97] sts.
Cont in st-st as follows:-
Work 2[4:4:6:8] rows.
**Next row. (ws)** P2tog, purl to last 2 sts, p2togtbl. 69[77:87:95:95] sts.
**Next row.** S1, k1, psso, knit to last 2 sts, k2tog. 67[75:85:93:93] sts.
**Next row.** P2tog, purl to last 2 sts, p2togtbl. 65[73:83:91:91] sts.
Break off yarn.
**Collar Edging**
With rs facing, join yarn to pick up sts at right side of collar and using 3¼ mm needles pick up and knit 6[8:8:10:12] sts up right side of collar, 4 sts around curved edge of collar, then knit across 65[73:83:91:91] sts left on the 4 mm needle, pick up and knit 4 sts around the curved edge and 6[8:8:10:12] sts down left side of collar. 85[97:107:119:123] sts.
Work 4 rows in g-st.
Cast off knitways (on **ws**).

**BELT**
Using 4 mm needles and thumb method cast on 21[23:25:27:29] sts.
Work 12[12:14:14:14] rows in moss-st.
Cast off in moss-st.
Sew to back of Jacket placing 1 button at each side.

**TO MAKE UP**
Fold sleeves in half lengthways and placing folds to shoulder seams sew sleeves in position. Join side and sleeve seams. Sew on buttons. Pin out coat to the measurements given. Cover with clean, damp tea towels and leave to dry. See ball band for washing and further care instructions.

*Little Mandarin Coat*
**BACK**
Work as given for Back of Willow Coat.

## LEFT FRONT
Work as given for Left Front of Willow Coat.

## RIGHT FRONT
Work as given for Right Front of Willow Coat.

## SLEEVES (Both alike)
Work as given for Sleeves of Willow Coat.

## COLLAR
Join shoulder seams.
Using 3¼ mm needles, beg halfway between buttonholes, pick up and knit 19[19:24:24:24] sts evenly up right side of neck, 19[23:23:27:27] sts from back of neck and 19[19:24:24:24] sts evenly down left side of neck, ending halfway between button markers. 57[61:71:75:75] sts.
Work 8[8:10:12:14] rows in g-st.
Cast off knitways (on **ws**).

## TO MAKE UP
Make Up as given for Willow Coat.

# Little Heart Jersey & Little Star Hoodie

## MEASUREMENTS

### Ages

| Mths | 0-9 | 9-18 | 18-24 | 3-5 years | 5-7 years |
|---|---|---|---|---|---|

### To Fit Chest

| | | | | | |
|---|---|---|---|---|---|
| cm | 41-46 | 46-51 | 51-56 | 56-61 | 61-66 |
| in | 16-18 | 18-20 | 20-22 | 22-24 | 24-26 |

### Actual Measurement

| | | | | | |
|---|---|---|---|---|---|
| cm | 50 | 56 | 61 | 67 | 73 |
| in | 19¾ | 22 | 24 | 26½ | 28¾ |

### Full Length

| | | | | | |
|---|---|---|---|---|---|
| cm | 26 | 30 | 36 | 40 | 44 |
| in | 10¼ | 11¾ | 14 | 15¾ | 17¼ |

### Sleeve Length

| | | | | | |
|---|---|---|---|---|---|
| cm | 16 | 19 | 23 | 28 | 32 |
| in | 6¼ | 7½ | 9 | 11 | 12½ |

## MATERIALS

**Little Heart Jersey** Cottonsoft DK

| | | | | | | |
|---|---|---|---|---|---|---|
| A Shade 712 Rose | 100g balls | 1A | 2A | 2A | 3A | 3A |
| B shade 710 White | | 1B | 1B | 1B | 1B | 1B |

**Little Star Hoodie** Baby Alpaca DK

| | | | | | | |
|---|---|---|---|---|---|---|
| A shade 501 Fawn | 50g balls | 2A | 3A | 4A | 5A | 6A |
| B shade 502 Grey | | 1B | 2B | 2B | 2B | 3B |

Also suitable for any King Cole DK yarns.
It is essential to work to the stated tension to achieve the correct size of garment.

## Needles
1 pair 4 mm (UK 8 – USA 6) knitting needles
1 pair 3¼ mm (UK 10 – USA 3) knitting needles

## Tension
22 sts and 28 rows to 10 cm, 4 in over stocking stitch on 4 mm needles or the size required to give the correct tension.

# Little Heart Jersey

## BACK
Using 3¼ mm needles, yarn A and thumb method cast on 66[70:78:86:94] sts.
**1st row.** * K2, p2, rep from * to last 2 sts, k2.
**2nd row.** * P2, k2, rep from * to last 2 sts, p2.
These 2 rows are called **2x2 rib**.
Work 5 [5:7:7:7] rows more in rib.
**Next row.** P2[6:3:6:4], p2tog, (p4[5:5:4:5], p2tog) 10[8:10:12:12] times, p2[6:3:6:4]. 55[61:67:73:81] sts.
Change to 4 mm needles and work as follows:-
**1st row.** Knit.
**2nd row.** Purl.

These 2 rows are called **st-st** (stocking stitch).
Work in st-st (throughout) until back measures 8[11:16:19:22] cm, 3[4¼:6¼:7½:8¾] in, ending with a ws row. **
Work 14 rows more.
**Shape Raglan**
Cast off 2[3:3:3:3] sts at beg of next 2 rows. 51[55:61:67:75] sts.
**For 1st and 2nd sizes only**
Work 4 rows dec 1 st at each end of 1st row. 49[53] sts.
**For 3rd, 4th and 5th sizes only**
Work 2[2:6] rows dec 1 st at each end of every row. [57:63:63] sts.
**For all sizes**
Work 24[26:30:32:32] rows dec 1

st at each end of next and every foll alt row. 25[27:27:31:31] sts.
Leave rem 25[27:27:31:31] sts on a stitch holder.

## FRONT

**Pattern note:** using a separate ball of wool for each colour, twist the new colour to be used with the colour just finished to prevent a hole forming. This is called **intarsia**.

Work as given for Back to **.
Work in patt as follows:-
**1st row.** K27[30:33:36:40]A, k1B, k27[30:33:36:40]A.
**2nd row.** P27[30:33:36:40]A, p1B, p27[30:33:36:40]A.
**3rd row.** K26[29:32:35:39]A, k3B, k26[29:32:35:39]A.
**4th row.** P26[29:32:35:39]A, p3B, p26[29:32:35:39]A.
**5th row.** K25[28:31:34:38]A, k5B, k25[28:31:34:38]A.
**6th row.** P25[28:31:34:38]A, p5B, p25[28:31:34:38]A.
**7th row.** K24[27:30:33:37]A, k7B, k24[27:30:33:37]A.
**8th row.** P24[27:30:33:37]A, p7B, p24[27:30:33:37]A.
**9th row.** K23[26:29:32:36]A, k9B, k23[26:29:32:36]A.
**10th row.** P23[26:29:32:36]A, p9B, p23[26:29:32:36]A.
**11th row.** K22[25:28:31:35]A, k11B, k22[25:28:31:35]A.
**12th row.** P22[25:28:31:35]A, p11B, p22[25:28:31:35]A.
**13th row.** K21[24:27:30:34]A, k13B, k21[24:27:30:34]A.
**14th row.** P21[24:27:30:34]A, p13B, p21[24:27:30:34]A.
**Shape Raglan**
**15th row.** Using A cast off 2[3:3:3:3] sts, k17[19:22:25:29]A, k15B, k20[23:26:29:33]A. 53[58:64:70:78] sts.
**16th row.** Using A cast off 2[3:3:3:3] sts, p17[19:22:25:29]A, p15B, p18[20:23:26:30]A. 51[55:61:67:75] sts.
**17th row.** K2tog A, k15[17:20:23:27]A, k17B, k15[17:20:23:27]A, k2togA. 49[53:59:65:73] sts.
**18th row.** (P2togA) 0[0:1:1:1] times, p16[18:19:22:26]A, p17B, p16[18:19:22:26]A, (p2togA) 0[0:1:1:1] times. 49[53:57:63:71] sts.
**19th row.** (K2togA) 0 [0:1:1:1] times, k17[19:19:22:26]A, k7B, k1A, k7B, k17[19:19:22:26]A, (k2togA) 0[0:1:1:1] times. 49[53:55:61:69] sts.
**20th row.** (P2togA) 0[0:0:0:1] times, p17[19:20:23:25]A, p7B, p1A, p7B, p17[19:20:23:25]A, (p2togA) 0[0:0:0:1] times. 49[53:55:61:67] sts.
**21st row.** K2togA, k16[18:19:22:25]A, k5B, k3A, k5B, k16[18:19:22:25]A, k2togA. 47[51:53:59:65] sts.
**22nd row.** (P2togA) 0[0:0:0:1] times, p17[19:20:23:24]A, p5B, p3A, p5B, p17[19:20:23:24]A, (p2togA) 0[0:0:0:1] times. 47[51:53:59:63] sts.
*** Work in yarn A only throughout as follows:-
Work 10[12:12:14:18] rows dec 1 st at each end of next and every foll alt row. 37[39:41:45:45] sts.
**Shape Neck**
**Next row.** K2tog, k11[11:13:13:13], turn and leave rem 24[26:26:30:30] sts on a stitch holder. Working on rem 12[12:14:14:14] sts only proceed as follows:-
**Next row.** Purl.
Work 2 rows dec 1 st at raglan edge in 1st row **AT THE SAME TIME** dec 1 st at neck edge in every row. 9[9:11:11:11] sts.
Work 4[4:6:6:6] rows dec 1 st at each end of next and every foll alt row. 5 sts.
Work 3 rows dec 1 st at raglan edge in next and foll alt row **AT THE SAME TIME** dec 1 st at neck edge in 1st row. 2 sts.
**Next row.** P2tog, fasten off.
With rs facing, working on rem 24[26:26:30:30] sts left on a stitch holder cast off next 11[13:11:15:15] sts, rejoin yarn A and knit to last 2 sts, k2tog. 12[12:14:14:14] sts.
**Next row.** Purl.
Work 2 rows dec 1 st at neck edge in every row **AT THE**

**SAME TIME** dec 1 st at raglan edge in 1st row. 9[9:11:11:11] sts.
Work 4[4:6:6:6] rows dec 1 st at each end of next and every foll alt row. 5 sts.
Work 3 rows dec 1 st at neck edge in 1st row **AT THE SAME TIME** dec 1 st at raglan edge in next and foll alt row. 2 sts.
**Next row.** P2tog, fasten off.

## SLEEVES (Both alike)

Using 3¼ mm needles, yarn A and thumb method cast on 38[38:38:42:46] sts.
Work 7[7:9:9:9] rows in 2x2 rib as given for Back.
**Next row.** P3[6:6:4:1], p2tog, (p3[4:4:6:5], p2tog) 6[4:4:4:6] times, p3[6:6:4:1]. 31[33:33:37:39] sts.
Change to 4 mm needles and work in st-st (throughout) inc 1 st at each end of 5th[5th:5th:5th:7th] and every foll 6th[6th:6th:8th:8th] row to 35[43:49:53:57] sts.
**For 1st and 2nd sizes only**
Inc 1 st at each end of every foll 8th row to 39[45] sts.
**For all sizes**
Cont without shaping until sleeve measures 16[19:23:28:32] cm, 6¼[7½:9:11:12½] in, ending with a ws row.
**Shape Raglan**
Cast off 2[3:3:3:3] sts at beg of next 2 rows. 35[39:43:47:51] sts.
**For 1st, 2nd and 3rd sizes only**
Work 8[8:4] rows dec 1 st at each end of next and foll 4th[4th:0] row. 31[35:41] sts.
**For all sizes**
Work 20[22:28:34:38] rows dec 1 st at each end of next and every foll alt row. 11[13:13:13:13] sts.
Leave rem 11[13:13:13:13] sts on a stitch holder.

## NECKBAND

Join raglan seams leaving left back raglan open.
With rs facing, using 3¼ mm needles and yarn A, knit across

11[13:13:13:13] sts left on a stitch holder at top of left sleeve, pick up and knit 10[10:13:13:13] sts evenly down left side of neck, 11[13:11:15:15] sts at front of neck, 10[10:13:13:13] sts evenly up right side of neck, knit across 11[13:13:13:13] sts left on a stitch holder at top of right sleeve and 25[27:27:31:31] sts left on a stitch holder at back of neck. 78[86:90:98:98] sts.
Beg with 2nd row of 2x2 rib as given for Back, work 7 [7:9:9:9] rows.
Cast off in rib.

## TO MAKE UP
Join left back raglan and neckband seams. Join side and sleeve seams. Pin out Jersey to the measurement given. Cover with clean, damp tea towels and leave until dry. See ball band for washing and further care instructions.

## Little Star Hoodie
### BACK
Work as given for Back of Little Heart Jersey casting off rem 25[27:27:31:31]sts.

### FRONT
**Pattern note:** using a separate ball of wool for each colour, twist the new colour to be used with the colour just finished to prevent a hole forming. This is called **intarsia**.

Work as given for Back of Little Heart Jersey to **.
Work in patt as follows:-
**1st row.** K27[30:33:36:40]A, k1B, k27[30:33:36:40]A.
**2nd row.** P27[30:33:36:40]A, p1B, p27[30:33:36:40]A.
**3rd row.** K26[29:32:35:39]A, k3B, k26[29:32:35:39]A.
**4th row.** P26[29:32:35:39]A, p3B, p26[29:32:35:39]A.
**5th row.** K25[28:31:34:38]A, k5B, k25[28:31:34:38]A.

**6th row.** P25[28:31:34:38]A, p5B, p25[28:31:34:38]A.
**7th row.** K20[23:26:29:33]A, k15B, k20[23:26:29:33]A.
**8th row.** P20[23:26:29:33]A, p15B, p20[23:26:29:33]A.
**9th row.** K21[24:27:30:34]A, k13B, k21[24:27:30:34]A.
**10th row.** P21[24:27:30:34]A, p13B, p21[24:27:30:34]A.
**11th row.** K22[25:28:31:35]A, k11B, k22[25:28:31:35]A.
**12th row.** P22[25:28:31:35]A, p11B, p22[25:28:31:35]A.
**13th row.** As 9th row
**14th row.** As 10th row.
**Shape Raglan**
**15th row.** Using A cast off 2[3:3:3:3] sts, k17[19:22:25:29]A, k15B, k20[23:26:29:33]A. 53[58:64:70:78] sts.
**16th row.** Using A cast off 2[3:3:3:3] sts, p17[19:22:25:29]A, p15B, p18[20:23:26:30]A. 51[55:61:67:75] sts.
**17th row.** K2togA, k21[23:26:29:33]A, k5B, k21[23:26:29:33]A, k2togA. 49[53:59:65:73] sts.
**18th row.** (P2togA) 0[0:1:1:1] times, p22[24:25:28:32]A, p5B, p22[24:25:28:32]A, (p2togA) 0[0:1:1:1] times. 49[53:57:63:71] sts.
**19th row.** (K2togA) 0[0:1:1:1] times, k23[25:25:28:32]A, k3B, k23[25:25:28:32]A, (k2togA) 0[0:1:1:1] times. 49[53:55:61:69] sts.
**20th row.** (P2togA) 0[0:0:0:1]

times, p23[25:26:29:31]A, p3B, p23[25:26:29:31]A, (p2togA) 0[0:0:0:1] times. 49[53:55:61:67] sts.
**21st row.** K2togA, k22[24:25:28:31]A, k1B, k22[24:25:28:31]A, k2togA. 47[51:53:59:65] sts.
**22nd row.** (P2togA) 0[0:0:0:1] times, p23[25:26:29:30]A, p1B, p23[25:26:29:30]A, (p2togA) 0[0:0:0:1] times. 47[51:53:59:63] sts.
Complete as given for Front of Jersey from ***.

## SLEEVES (Both alike)
Work as given for Sleeves of Little Heart Jersey using B and casting off rem 11[13:13:13:13] sts at sleeve top.

## HOOD
Using 4 mm needles, yarn A and thumb method, cast on 68 [73:75: 79:81] sts.
Work in st-st until hood measures 18[19:20:21:22] cm, 7[7½:8:8¼:8¾] in, ending with a ws row.
**Shape Top**
**Next row.** Cast off 23[24:25:26:27] sts, k21[24:24:26:26], cast off rem 23[24:25:26:27] sts. 22[25:25:27:27] sts.
With ws facing, rejoin yarn to rem 22[25:25:27:27] sts and cont until hood measures 10.5[11:11.5: 12:12.5] cm, 4¼[4¼:4½:4¾:5] in, from cast off sts, ending with a ws row. Cast off.
Join sides of hood to 23[24:25:26:27] cast off sts.

## HOOD BORDER
With rs facing, using 3¼ mm needles and yarn A, pick up and knit 45[47:49:50:51] sts evenly along right side of hood, 24[24:24:26:28] sts from 22[25:25:27:27] cast off sts at top of hood and 45[47:49:50:51] sts evenly along left side of hood.

114[118:122:126:130] sts.
Beg with 2 nd row of 2x2 rib as given for Back, work 7[7:9:9:9] rows.
Cast off in rib.

**TO MAKE UP**
Join raglan seams. Placing front edges of hood at centre of front neck sew hood evenly in position all around neck edge and across sleeve tops. Join side and sleeve seams. Pin out hoodie to the measurement given. Cover with clean, damp tea towels and leave until dry. See ball band for washing and further care instructions.

# Little Sailor Hoodie & Little Pebble Body Warmer

## MEASUREMENTS

**Ages**

| Mths | 0-9 | 9-18 | 18-24 | 3-5 years | 5-7 years |
|---|---|---|---|---|---|
| **To Fit Chest** | | | | | |
| cm | 41-46 | 46-51 | 51-56 | 56-61 | 61-66 |
| in | 16-18 | 18-20 | 20-22 | 22-24 | 24-26 |
| **Actual Measurement** | | | | | |
| cm | 51 | 55 | 62 | 65 | 71 |
| in | 20 | 21¾ | 24½ | 25½ | 28 |
| **Full Length** | | | | | |
| cm | 28 | 32 | 38 | 42 | 48 |
| in | 11 | 12½ | 15 | 16½ | 19 |
| **Sleeve Length** | | | | | |
| cm | 16 | 19 | 23 | 28 | 32 |
| in | 6¼ | 7½ | 9 | 11 | 12½ |

## MATERIALS

**Little Sailor Hoodie** Bamboo Cotton DK

| | | | | | | |
|---|---|---|---|---|---|---|
| A 634 Crimson | 100g balls | 1A | 1A | 1A | 1A | 1A |
| B 543 Oyster | | 2B | 2B | 2B | 3B | 3B |
| C 525 Cobalt | | 1C | 1C | 1C | 1C | 1C |

**Little Pebble Body Warmer** Baby Alpaca DK

| | | | | | | |
|---|---|---|---|---|---|---|
| A 502 Grey | 50g balls | 1A | 1A | 1A | 2A | 2A |
| B 501 Fawn | | 2B | 2B | 3B | 4B | 4B |
| C 504 Koala | | 1C | 1C | 1C | 2C | 2C |

Also suitable for any King Cole DK yarns.
It is essential to work to the stated tension to achieve the correct size of garment.

**Needles**
1 pair 3¼ mm (UK10 – USA3 ) knitting needles
1 pair 4 mm (UK8 – USA6) knitting needles
5[5:6:6:6] Buttons for Hoodie
5 Buttons for Body Warmer

**Tension**
22sts and 28 rows to 10cm, 4 in over stocking-stitch using 4mm needles or the size required to give the correct tension.

## Little Sailor Hoodie

### BACK
Using 3¼ mm needles, thumb method and yarn A, cast on 66[70:78:86:90] sts.
**1st row.** * K2, p2, rep from * to last 2 sts, k2.
**2nd row.** * P2, k2, rep from * to last 2 sts, p2.
These 2 rows are called **2x2 rib**.
Work 7 rows more in rib.
**10th row.** P5[7:6:3:5], p2tog, (p4[4:5:4:5], p2tog) 9[9:9:13:11] times, p5[7:7:3:6]. 56[60:68:72:78] sts.
Change to 4mm needles.
**1st row.** Knit.
**2nd row.** Purl.
These 2 rows are called **st-st** (stocking-stitch).
Work in st-st (throughout) as follows:
Cont until back measures 10[11: 13:14:16] cm, 4[4¼:5¼:5½:6¼] in, ending with a ws row.
Change to yarn B and cont until back measures 28[32:38:42:48] cm, 11[12½:15:16½:19] in, ending with a ws row.

### Shape Shoulders
Cast off 6[6:7:7:8] sts at beg of next 2 rows. 44[48:54:58:62] sts.
Cast off 6[6:8:8:9] sts at beg of next 2 rows. 32[36:38:42:44] sts.
Cast off 6[7:8:8:9] sts at beg of next 2 rows. 20[22:22:26:26] sts.
Cast off rem 20[22:22:26:26] sts.

### LEFT FRONT
Using 3¼ mm needles, yarn A and thumb method, cast on 27[31:35: 39:43] sts.
**1st row.** * K2, p2, rep from * to last 3 sts, k2, p1.
**2nd row.** K1, p2, * k2, p2, rep from * to end.
These 2 rows form **rib**.
Work 7 rows more in rib.
**10th row.** P7[3:5:4:3], p2tog, (p10[6:6:4:4], p2tog) 1[3:3:5:6] times, p6[2:4:3:2]. 25[27:31:33:36] sts.
Change to 4 mm needles. Work in st-st (throughout) as follows:
Cont until left front measures 10[11:13:14:16] cm, 4[4¼:5¼:5½:6¼] in, ending with a ws row.

Change to yarn B and cont until left front measures 25[29:34:38:44] cm, 9¾[11½:13½:15:17¼] in, ending with a rs row.

### Shape Neck
**Next row.** Cast off 4[5:4:6:6] sts, purl to end. 21[22:27:27:30] sts.
Work 3[3:2:2:2] rows dec 1

st at neck edge in every row. 18[19:25:25:28] sts.
**For 3rd, 4th and 5th sizes only**
Work 3 rows dec 1 st at neck edge in next and foll alt row. [23:23:26] sts.
**For all sizes**
Cont without shaping until left front measures 28[32:38:42:48] cm, 11[12½:15:16½:19] in, ending with a ws row.
**Shape Shoulder**
**Next row.** Cast off 6[6:7:7:8] sts, knit to end. 12[13:16:16:18] sts.
**Next row.** Purl.
**Next row.** Cast off 6[6:8:8:9] sts, knit to end. 6[7:8:8:9] sts.
**Next row.** Purl.
Cast off rem 6[7:8:8:9] sts.

## RIGHT FRONT
Using 3¼ mm needles, yarn A and thumb method, cast on 27[31:35: 39:43] sts.
**1st row.** P1, * k2, p2, rep from * to last 2 sts, k2.
**2nd row.** P2, * k2, p2, rep from * to last st, k1.
These 2 rows form **rib.**
Work 7 rows more in rib.
**10th row.** P6[2:4:3:2], p2tog, (p10[6:6:4:4], p2tog) 1[3:3:5:6] times, p7[3:5:4:3]. 25[27:31:33:36] sts.
Change to 4 mm needles. Work in st-st (throughout) as follows:-
Cont until right front measures 10[11:13:14:16] cm, 4[4¼:5¼: 5½:6¼] in, ending with a ws row.
Change to yarn B and cont until right front measures 25[29:34: 38:44] cm, 9¾[11½:13½:15:17¼] in, ending with a ws row.
**Shape Neck**
**Next row.** Cast off 4[5:4:6:6] sts, knit to end. 21[22:27:27:30] sts.
**Next row.** Purl.
Work 3[3:2:2:2] rows dec 1 st at neck edge in every row. 18[19:25:25:28] sts.
**For 3rd, 4th and 5th sizes only**
Work 3 rows dec 1 st at neck edge in next and foll alt row. [23:23:26] sts.

**For all sizes**
Cont without shaping until back measures 28[32:38:42:48] cm, 11[12½:15:16½:19] in, ending with a rs row.
**Shape Shoulder**
**Next row.** Cast off 6[6:7:7:8] sts, purl to end. 12[13:16:16:18] sts.
**Next row.** Knit.
**Next row.** Cast off 6[6:8:8:9] sts, purl to end. 6[7:8:8:9] sts.
**Next row.** Knit.
Cast off rem 6[7:8:8:9] sts.

## SLEEVES (Both alike)
Using 3¼ mm needles, yarn A and thumb method, cast on 38[38:38:42:46] sts.
Work 9 rows in 2x2 rib as given for Back.
**10th row.** P3[6:6:8:2], p2tog, (p4[6:6:6:6], p2tog) 5[3:3:3:5] times, p3[6:6:8:2]. 32[34:34:38:40] sts
Change to 4 mm needles and yarn C.
Work in st-st (throughout) as folls:
Inc 1 st at each end of 5th and every foll 4th[4th:4th:6th:6th] row to 44[42:50:58:56] sts.
**For 2nd, 3rd and 5th sizes only**
Inc 1 st at each end of every foll [6th:6th:8th] row to[48:54:62] sts.
**For all sizes**
Cont without shaping until sleeve measures 16[19:23:28:32] cm, 6¼[7½:9:11:12½] in, ending with a ws row.
**Shape Top**
Cast off 4[3:3:3:3] sts at beg of next 6[2:4:8:12] rows. 20[42:42:34:26] sts.
Cast off 5[4:4:4:4] sts at beg of next 2[8:8:6:4] rows. 10 sts.
Cast off rem 10 sts.

## LEFT FRONT BORDER
With rs facing, using 3¼ mm needles and yarn B, pick up and knit 59[67:83:91:107] sts evenly along left front edge and 7 sts from rib. 66[74:90:98:114] sts.
Beg with 2nd row of 2x2 rib,

work 3 rows.
**Next row.** Rib 4[4:4:3:4], cast off 1 st, (rib 12[14:14:16:19], cast off 1 st) 4[4:5:5:5] times, rib 4[4:4:3:3].
**Next row.** Rib 5[5:5:4:4], cast on 1 st, (rib 13[15:15:17:20], cast on 1 st) 4[4:5:5:5] times, rib 4[4:4:3:4].
Work 4 rows more in rib.
Cast off in rib.

## RIGHT FRONT BORDER
With rs facing, using 3¼ mm needles and yarn B, pick up and knit 7 sts from rib and 59[67:83:91:107] sts evenly along right front edge. 66[74:90:98:114] sts.
Beg with 2nd row of 2x2 rib, work 9 rows.
Cast off in rib.

## HOOD
Using 4mm needles, yarn B and thumb method, cast on 66 [70:75: 79:81] sts.
Work in st-st until hood measures 18[19:20:21:22] cm, 7[7½:8:8¼:8¾] in, ending with a ws row.
**Shape Top**
Cast off 22[23:25:26:27] sts, k21[23:24:26:26], cast off 22[23:25:26:27] sts. 22[24:25:27:27] sts.
With ws facing, rejoin yarn to rem 22[24:25:27:27] sts and cont until hood measures 9.5[10.5:11.5: 12:12.5] cm, 3¾[4¼:4½:4¾:5] in, from cast off sts, ending with a ws row.
Cast off.
Join sides of hood to cast off sts.

## HOOD BORDER
With rs facing, using 3¼ mm needles and yarn B, pick up and knit 45[47:49:50:51] sts evenly along right side of hood, 24[24:24:26:28] sts from 22[24:25:27:27] cast off sts at top of hood and 45[47:49:50:51] sts evenly along left side of hood.

114[118:122:126:130] sts.
Beg with 2 row of 2x2 rib, work 9 rows.
Cast off in rib.

## SLEEVE TAB
Using 3¼ mm needles, yarn C and thumb method, cast on 14[14:18:18:18] sts.
Work 8 rows in 2x2 rib.
Cast off in rib.

## Ears (Make 4 pieces)
Using 4 mm needles, A and thumb method cast on 12 sts.
Starting with a k row, work in st-st throughout as follows:-
Work 6 rows, ending with a ws row. Dec 1 st at each end of next and foll alt row, then on foll row, ending with a ws row.
Cast off rem 6 sts.
With right sides facing, sew 2 ear pieces together (to make each ear) leaving cast on edges open.

## TO MAKE UP
Join shoulder seams. Fold sleeves in half lengthways and placing folds to shoulder seams sew sleeves in position 12[13:14:15:16] cm, 4¾[5¼:5½:6:6¼]in, from shoulder seams.
Join side and sleeve seams.

Placing front edges of hood at centre of front neck sew hood in position. Sew on buttons. Sew tab to Left sleeve. Sew on ears in position as shown on pages 18/19. Pin out hoodie to the measurement given. Cover with clean, damp tea towels and leave until dry. See ball band for washing and further care instructions.

# Little Pebble Body Warmer

## BACK
Work as given for Back of Little Sailor Hoodie.

## LEFT FRONT
Work as given for Left Front of Little Sailor Hoodie.

## RIGHT FRONT
Work as given for Right Front of Little Sailor Hoodie.

## LEFT FRONT BORDER
Using C, work as given for Left Front Border of Little Sailor Hoodie.

## RIGHT FRONT BORDER
Using C, work as given for Right Front Border of Little Sailor Hoodie.

## HOOD
Using B Work as given for Hood of Little Sailor Hoodie.

## HOOD BORDER
Using C, work as given for Hood Border of Little Sailor Hoodie.

## ARMHOLE BORDERS (Both alike)
Join shoulder seams.
Place markers 12[13:14:15:16] cm, 4¾[5¼:5½:6:6¼]in, from shoulder seams.
With rs facing, using 3¼ mm needles and yarn C, pick up and knit 58[62:66:70:74] sts between markers.
Beg with 2nd row of 2x2 rib, work 10 rows.
Cast off in rib.

## TO MAKE UP
Join side and armhole border seams. Placing front edges of hood at centre of front neck sew hood in position. Sew on buttons. Pin out Body Warmer to the measurement given. Cover with clean, damp tea towels and leave until dry. See ball band for washing and further care instructions.

# Little Surfer Jacket & Little Lumber Jacket

## MEASUREMENTS

### Ages

| Mths | 6-12 months | 1-2 years | 2-3 years | 4-5 years | 6-7 years |
|---|---|---|---|---|---|
| **To Fit Chest** | | | | | |
| cm | 46 | 51 | 56 | 61 | 66 |
| in | 18 | 20 | 22 | 24 | 26 |
| **Actual Measurement** | | | | | |
| cm | 51 | 56 | 62 | 67 | 72 |
| in | 20 | 22 | 24½ | 26½ | 28¼ |
| **Full Length** | | | | | |
| cm | 28 | 32 | 38 | 42 | 48 |
| in | 11 | 12½ | 15 | 16½ | 19 |
| **Sleeve Length** | | | | | |
| cm | 16 | 19 | 23 | 28 | 32 |
| in | 6¼ | 7½ | 9 | 11 | 12½ |

## MATERIALS

**Little Surfer Jacket**
Bamboo Cotton DK

| | | | | | | |
|---|---|---|---|---|---|---|
| shade 522 Grey | 100g balls | 2 | 2 | 3 | 3 | 4 |

**Little Lumber Jacket**
Merino Blend DK

| | | | | | | |
|---|---|---|---|---|---|---|
| Shade 857 Bark | 50g balls | 3 | 4 | 5 | 7 | 8 |

Also suitable for any King Cole DK yarns.
It is essential to work to the stated tension to achieve the correct size of garment.

**Needles**
1 pair 5½ mm (UK 5 – USA 9) knitting needles for Shawl Collared Jacket
1 pair 4 mm (UK 8 – USA 6) knitting needles
1 pair 3¼ mm (UK 10 – USA 3) knitting needles
5[5:5:6:6] buttons

**Tension**
22 sts and 28 rows to 10 cm, 4 in, over stocking stitch on 4 mm needles or the size required to give the correct tension.
Check your tension – if less stitches use thinner needles, if more use thicker needles.

# Little Surfer Jacket

## BACK

Using 3¼ mm needles and thumb method cast on 66[70:78:86:94] sts.

**1st row.** * K2, p2, rep from * to last 2 sts, k2.

**2nd row.** P2, * k2, p2, rep from * to end.

These 2 rows are called **2x2 rib**. Work 7 rows more in 2x2 rib.

**10th row.** P4[6:6:6:4], p2tog, (p5[5:6:4:4], p2tog) 8[8:8:12:14] times, p4[6:6:6:4]. 57[61:69:73:79] sts.

Change to 4 mm needles and work as follows:-

**1st row.** Knit.

**2nd row.** Purl.

Last 2 rows form **st-st** (stocking stitch).

Cont in st-st until back measures 28[32:38:42:48] cm, 11[12½:15:16½:19] in, ending with a ws row.

### Shape Shoulders

Cast off 8[9:11:11:12] sts at beg of next 2 rows. 41[43:47:51:55] sts.

Cast off 9[9:11:11:13] sts at beg of next 2 rows. 23[25:25:29:29] sts.

Cast off rem 23[25:25:29:29] sts.

## LEFT FRONT

Using 3¼ mm needles and thumb method cast on 31[35:39:43:47] sts.

**1st row.** * K2, p2, rep from * to last 3 sts, k2, p1.

**2nd row.** K1, p2, * k2, p2, rep from * to end.

1st and 2nd rows form **rib**. Work 7 rows more in rib.

**10th row.** P3[5:4:5:23], m1, (p4[6:10:16:0], m1) 6[4:3:2:0] times, p4[6:5:6:24]. 38[40:43:46:48] sts.

Change to 4 mm needles and work as follows:-

**1st row.** K0[2:5:6:8], p2, k12, p2, k3[3:3:5:5], p2, k12, p2, k3.

**2nd row.** P3, k2, p12, k2, p3[3:3:5:5], k2, p12, k2, p0[2:5:6:8].

**3rd row.** K0[2:5:6:8], p2, slip next 3 sts onto CN and hold at back of work, k3 then k3 from CN, this will now be called **C6B**, slip next 3 sts onto CN and hold at front of work, k3 then k3 from CN, this will now be called **C6F**, p2, k3[3:3:5:5], p2, C6B, C6F, p2, k3.

**4th row.** As 2nd row.

**5th row.** As 1st row.

**6th row.** P3, k2, p12, k2, p3[3:3:5:5], k2, p12, k2, p0[2:5:6:8].

From 1st to 6th row forms **patt**.

Cont in patt until left front measures 24[28:33:37:43] cm, 9½[11:13:14½:17] in, ending with a rs row.

### Shape Neck

**Next row.** Cast off 5[5:5:6:6] sts in patt, patt to end. 33[35:38:40:42] sts.

**Next row.** Patt to last 2 sts, patt2tog. 32[34:37:39:41] sts.

**Next row.** Cast off 5[6:5:7:6] sts in patt, patt to end. 27[28:32:32:35] sts.

Work 2 rows dec 1 st at neck edge in every row. 25[26:30:30:33] sts.

Work 3 rows dec 1 st at neck edge in next and foll alt row. 23[24:28:28:31] sts.

Cont without shaping until left front measures 28[32:38:42:48] cm, 11[12½:15:16½:19] in, ending with a rs row.

**Next row.** Patt 9[8:9:8:9], (p2tog) 6 times, patt 2[4:7:8:10]. 17[18:22:22:25] sts.

### Shape Shoulder

**Next row.** Cast off 8[9:11:11:12] sts in patt, patt to end. 9[9:11:11:13] sts.

**Next row.** Patt.

Cast off rem 9[9:11:11:13] sts in patt.

## RIGHT FRONT

Using 3¼ mm needles and thumb method cast on 31[35:39:43:47] sts.

**1st row.** P1, k2, * p2, k2, rep from * to end.

**2nd row.** * P2, k2, rep from * to last 3 sts, p2, k1.

1st and 2nd rows form **rib**. Work 7 rows more in rib.

**10th row.** P4[6:5:6:24], m1, (p4[6:10:16:0], m1) 6[4:3:2:0] times, p3[5:4:5:23]. 38[40:43:46:48] sts.

Change to 4 mm needles and work as follows:-

**1st row.** K3, p2, k12, p2, k3[3:3:5:5], p2, k12, p2, k0[2:5:6:8].

**2nd row.** P0[2:5:6:8], k2, p12, k2, p3[3:3:5:5], k2, p12, k2, p3.

**3rd row.** K3, p2, C6B, C6F, p2, k3[3:3:5:5], p2, C6B, C6F, p2, k0[2:5:6:8].

**4th row.** As 2nd row.

**5th row.** As 1st row.

**6th row.** P0[2:5:6:8], k2, p12, k2, p3[3:3:5:5], k2, p12, k2, p3.

From 1st to 6th row forms **patt**.

Cont in patt until right front measures 24[28:33:37:43] cm, 9½[11:13:14½:17] in, ending with a ws row.

## Shape Neck

**Next row.** Cast off 5[5:5:6:6] sts in patt, patt to end. 33[35:38:40:42] sts.

**Next row.** Patt to last 2 sts, patt2tog. 32[34:37:39:41] sts.

**Next row.** Cast off 5[6:5:7:6] sts in patt, patt to end. 27[28:32:32:35] sts.

**Next row.** Patt.

Work 2 rows dec 1 st at neck edge in every row. 25[26:30:30:33] sts.

Work 3 rows dec 1 st at neck edge in next and foll alt row. 23[24:28:28:31] sts.

Cont without shaping until right front measures 28[32:38:42:48] cm, 11[12½:15:16½:19] in, ending with a ws row.

**Next row.** Patt 9[8:9:8:9], (k2tog) 6 times, patt 2[4:7:8:10]. 17[18:22:22:25] sts.

## Shape Shoulder

**Next row.** Cast off 8[9:11:11:12] sts in patt, patt to end. 9[9:11:11:13] sts.

**Next row.** Patt.

Cast off rem 9[9:11:11:13] sts in patt.

## SLEEVES (Both alike)

Using 3¼ mm needles and thumb method cast on 34[38:38:42:46] sts and work 9 rows in 2x2 rib as given for Back.

**10th row.** P6[4:4:6:4], p2tog, (p8[5:5:5:4], p2tog) 2[4:4:4:6] times, p6[4:4:6:4]. 31[33:33:37:39] sts.

Change to 4 mm needles and cont in st-st inc 1 st at each end of 3rd and every foll 4th[4th:4th:6th:6th] row to 45[45:45:53:53] sts.

**For 2nd, 3rd, 4th and 5th sizes only**

Inc 1 st at each end of every foll [6th:6th:8th:8th] row to [49:53:57:61] sts.

**For all sizes**

Cont without shaping until sleeve measures 16[19:23:28:32] cm, 6¼[7½:9:11:12½] in, ending with a ws row.

## Shape Sleeve Top

Cast off 4[4:3:3:3] sts at beg of next 6[2:6:2:6] rows. 21[41:35:51:43] sts.

Cast off 5[5:4:4:4] sts at beg of next 2[6:6:10:8] rows. 11 sts.

Cast off rem 11 sts.

## RIGHT FRONT BORDER

With rs facing, using 3¼ mm needles pick up and knit 9 sts evenly up rib and 49[57:69:81:93] sts evenly up front edge. 58[66:78:90:102] sts.

Beg with 2nd row of 2x2 rib as given for Back work 3 rows.

**For a Girl**

**Next row.** Rib 4[4:4:4:2], cast off 1 st, (rib 10[12:15:14:17], cast off 1 st) 4[4:4:5:5] times, rib 4[4:4:4:3].

**Next row.** Rib 5[5:5:5:4], cast on 1 st, (rib 11[13:16:15:18], cast on 1 st) 4[4:4:5:5] times, rib 4[4:4:4:2].

Work 4 rows more in 2x2 rib. Cast off in rib.

**For a Boy**

Work 6 rows more in 2x2 rib. Cast off in rib.

## LEFT FRONT BORDER

With rs facing, using 3¼ mm needles pick up and knit 49[57:69:81:93] sts evenly down front edge and 9 sts evenly down rib. 58[66:78:90:102] sts.

Beg with 2nd row of 2x2 rib as given for Back work 3 rows.

**For a Boy**

**Next row.** Rib 5[5:5:5:4], cast off 1 st, (rib 10[12:15:14:17], cast off 1 st) 4[4:4:5:5] times, rib 3[3:3:3:1].

**Next row.** Rib 4[4:4:4:2], cast on 1 st, (rib 11[13:16:15:18], cast on 1 st) 4[4:4:5:5] times, rib 5[5:5:5:4].

Work 4 rows more in 2x2 rib. Cast off in rib.

**For a Girl**

Work 6 rows more in 2x2 rib. Cast off in rib.

## NECKBAND

Join shoulder seams. With rs facing, using 3¼ mm needles pick up and knit 9 sts evenly across top of right front border, 25[26:28:28:28] sts evenly up right side of neck, 23[25:25:29:29] sts from back of neck, 24[25:27:27:27] sts evenly down left side of neck and 9 sts evenly across top of left front border. 90[94:98:102:102] sts.

Beg with 2nd row of 2x2 rib as given for Back work 4 rows.

**Next row.** Cast off 5 sts in rib, p2[1:3:2:2], (p2tog, p4) 12[13:13:14:14] times, p2tog, p3[2:4:3:3], rib 5. 72[75:79:82:82] sts.

**Next row.** Cast off 5 sts, knit to end. 67[70:74:77:77] sts.

Beg with 2nd row of st-st work 5 rows. Cast off.

## SLEEVE TAB

Using 3¼ mm needles and thumb method cast on 7 sts.

**1st row.** * K1, p1, rep from * to last st, k1.

**2nd row.** P1, * k1, p1, rep from * to end.

These 2 rows are called **1x1 rib**.

Cont in rib until tab measures 5 cm, 2 in, ending with a ws row. Cast off in rib.

## TO MAKE UP

Fold sleeves in half lengthways, then placing sleeve top folds to shoulder seams, sew sleeves in position for approximately 12[13:14:15:16] cm, 4¾[5¼:5½:6:6¼] in, from top of shoulders. Join side and sleeve seams. Sew on sleeve tab as illustrated. Sew on buttons. Pin out jacket to the measurement given. Cover with clean, damp tea towels and leave until dry. See ball band for washing and further care instructions.

## Little Lumber Jacket

Work as given for Little Surfer Jacket omitting Neckband and Making Up.

### COLLAR

Using 5½ mm needles, 2 ends of yarn tog and thumb method cast on 4 sts.

**1st row.** Knit.
This row is called **g-st** (garter stitch).

Work in g-st as follows:-
Work 9[9:15:24:24] rows inc 1 st at beg of 2nd and every foll alt row. 8[8:11:16:16] sts.

**For 1st, 2nd and 3rd sizes only**
Work 13[13:9] rows inc 1 st at beg of next and every foll 4th row. 12[12:14] sts.

**For all sizes**
Work 29[29:33:41:41] rows more without shaping.

**For 1st, 2nd and 3rd sizes only**

Work 13[13:9] rows dec 1 st at beg of next and every foll 4th row. 8[8:11] sts.

**For all sizes**
Work 10[10:16:24:24] rows dec 1 st at beg of next and every foll alt row. 4 sts.
Cast off.

### TO MAKE UP

Join shoulder seams. Fold sleeves in half lengthways, then placing sleeve top folds to shoulder seams, sew sleeves in position for approximately 12[13:14:15:16] cm, 4¾[5¼:5½:6:6¼] in, from top of shoulders. Join side and sleeve seams. Sew on sleeve tab as illustrated. Sew on buttons. Placing ends of collar halfway across front borders sew in position evenly all round neck edge. Pin out jacket to the measurement given. Cover with clean, damp tea towels and leave until dry. See ball band for washing and further care instructions.

## Little Holiday Cardie & Little Holiday Jacket

### MEASUREMENTS

**Ages**

| Mths | 0-9 | 9-18 | 18-24 | 3-5 years | 5-7 years |
|---|---|---|---|---|---|
| **To Fit Chest** | | | | | |
| cm | 41-46 | 46-51 | 51-56 | 56-61 | 61-66 |
| in | 16-18 | 18-20 | 20-22 | 22-24 | 24-26 |
| **Actual Measurement** | | | | | |
| cm | 50 | 55 | 61 | 66 | 72 |
| in | 19¾ | 21¾ | 24 | 26 | 28¼ |
| **Full Length** | | | | | |
| cm | 28 | 32 | 38 | 42 | 48 |
| in | 11 | 12½ | 15 | 16½ | 19 |
| **Sleeve Length** | | | | | |
| cm | 16 | 19 | 23 | 28 | 32 |
| in | 6¼ | 7½ | 9 | 11 | 12½ |

### MATERIALS

**Little Holiday Cardie**
Cottonsoft DK

| | | | | | | |
|---|---|---|---|---|---|---|
| shade 716 Candy | 100g balls | 2 | 2 | 2 | 3 | 4 |

**Little Holiday Jacket**
Bamboo Cotton DK

| | | | | | | |
|---|---|---|---|---|---|---|
| shade 518 Ice | 100g balls | 2 | 2 | 2 | 3 | 4 |

Also suitable for any King Cole DK yarns.
It is essential to work to the stated tension to achieve the correct size of garment.

**Needles**
1 pair 3¼ mm (UK 10 – USA 3) knitting needles
1 pair 4 mm (UK 8 - USA 6) knitting needles
2 Buttons for Round Neck Cardigan
3 Buttons for V Neck Cardigan

**Tension**
22 sts and 28 rows to 10cm, 4 in over stocking stitch, 22 sts and 30 rows over textured pattern and rib pattern, 21 sts and 34 rows over garter stitch ridge pattern using 4 mm needles or the size required to give the correct tension.

## Little Holiday Cardie

### BACK

Using 3¼ mm needles and thumb method cast on 55[61:67:73:79] sts.

**1st row.** Knit.
This row is called **g-st** (garter stitch).

Work 3 rows more in g-st.
Change to 4 mm needles and work as follows:-
**1st row.** * K1, p1, rep from * to last st, k1.
**2nd row.** * P1, k1, rep from * to last st, p1.

**3rd row.** Knit.
**4th row.** Purl.
**5th row.** As 2nd row.
**6th row.** As 1st row.
**7th & 8th rows.** As 3rd and 4th rows.
These 8 rows form **textured patt**.

Work 24[32:40:48:56] rows more in textured pattern dec 3 [3:3:4:4] sts evenly across last row.
52[58:64:69:75] sts.
**1st row.** Knit.
**2nd row.** Purl.
**3rd row.** Knit.
**4th row.** Knit.
These 4 rows form **g-st ridge patt**.
Work 24[28:32:36:40] rows more in g-st ridge patt inc 3[3:3:4:4] sts evenly across last row. 55[61:67:73:79] sts.
**1st row.** Knit.
**2nd row.** P1[0:0:2:1], k1[1:0:1:1], * p3, k1, rep from * to last 1[0:3:2:1] sts, p1[0:3:2:1].
These 2 rows form **rib patt**.
Cont in rib patt until back measures 28[32:38:42:48] cm, 11[12½:15:16½:19] in, ending with a ws row.
**Shape Shoulders**
Cast off 5[6:7:7:8] sts in patt at beg of next 4 rows.
35[37:39:45:47] sts.
Cast off 6[6:7:8:9] sts in patt at beg of next 2 rows.
23[25:25:29:29] sts.
Cast off rem 23[25:25:29:29] sts in patt.

**LEFT FRONT**
Using 3¼ mm needles and thumb method cast on 26[29:32:35:38] sts.
Work 4 rows in g-st as given for Back.
Change to 4 mm needles and work as follows:-
**1st row.** * K1, p1, rep from * to last 0[1:0:1:0] sts, k0[1:0:1:0].
**2nd row.** P0[1:0:1:0], * k1, p1, rep from * to end.
**3rd row.** Knit.
**4th row.** Purl.
**5th row.** * P1, k1, rep from * to last 0[1:0:1:0]sts, p0[1:0:1:0].
**6th row.** K0[1:0:1:0], * p1, k1, rep from * to end.
**7th row.** Knit.
**8th row.** Purl.
These 8 rows form **textured patt**.

Work 24[32:40:48:56] rows more in textured pattern dec 1[1:1:2:2] sts evenly across last row. 25[28:31:33:36] sts. **
Work 28[32:36:40:44] rows in g-st ridge patt as given for Back inc 1[1:1:2:2] sts evenly across last row. 26[29:32:35:38] sts.
**1st row.** Knit.
**2nd row.** K1, * p3, k1, rep from * to last 1[0:3:2:1] sts, p1[0:3:2:1].
These 2 rows form **rib patt**.
Cont in rib patt until left front measures 23[27:32:36:42] cm, 9[10¾:12½:14:16½] in, ending with a rs row.
**Shape Neck**
**Next row.** Cast off 4[5:5:7:7] sts in patt, patt to end.
22[24:27:28:31] sts.
Work 2 rows dec 1 st at neck edge in every row.
20[22:25:26:29] sts.
Work 4[4:2:2:2] rows dec 1 st at neck edge in next and foll alt[alt:0:0:0] row.
18[20:24:25:28] sts.
Work 5[5:9:9:9] rows dec 1 st at neck edge in next and every foll 4th row. 16[18:21:22:25] sts.
Cont in rib patt until left front measures 28[32:38:42:48] cm, 11[12½:15:16½:19] in, ending with a ws row.
**Shape Shoulder**
**Next row.** Cast off 5[6:7:7:8] sts in patt, patt to end.

11[12:14:15:17] sts.
**Next row.** Patt.
**Next row.** Cast off 5[6:7:7:8] sts in patt, patt to end. 6[6:7:8:9] sts.
**Next row.** Patt.
Cast off rem 6[6:7:8:9] sts in patt.

**RIGHT FRONT**
Using 3¼ mm needles and thumb method cast on 26[29:32:35:38] sts.
Work 4 rows in g-st as given for Back.
Change to 4 mm needles and work as follows:-
**1st row.** K0[1:0:1:0], * p1, k1, rep from * to end.
**2nd row.** * P1, k1, rep from * to last 0[1:0:1:0] sts, p0[1:0:1:0].
**3rd row.** Knit.
**4th row.** Purl.
**5th row.** P0[1:0:1:0], * k1, p1, rep from * to end.
**6th row.** * K1, p1, rep from * to last 0[1:0:1:0] sts, k0[1:0:1:0].
**7th row.** Knit.
**8th row.** Purl.
These 8 rows form **textured patt**.
Work 24[32:40:48:56] rows more in textured pattern dec 1[1:1:2:2] sts evenly across last row.
25[28:31:33:36] sts. **
Work 28[32:36:40:44] rows in g-st ridge patt as given for Back, inc 1[1:1:2:2] sts evenly across last row. 26[29:32:35:38] sts.
**1st row.** Knit.
**2nd row.** P1[0:0:2:1], k1[1:0:1:1], * p3, k1, rep from * to end.
These 2 rows form **rib patt**.
Cont in rib patt until right front measures 23[27:32:36:42] cm, 9[10¾:12½:14:16½] in, ending with a ws row.
**Shape Neck**
**Next row.** Cast off 4[5:5:7:7] sts in patt, patt to end.
22[24:27:28:31] sts.
**Next row.** Patt.
Work 2 rows dec 1 st at

neck edge in every row.
20[22:25:26:29] sts.
Work 4[4:2:2:2] rows dec
1 st at neck edge in next
and foll alt[alt:0:0:0] row.
18[20:24:25:28] sts.
Work 5[5:9:9:9] rows dec 1 st at
neck edge in next and every foll
4th row. 16[18:21:22:25] sts.
Cont in rib patt until right front
measures 28[32:38:42:48] cm,
11[12½:15:16½:19] in, ending
with a rs row.

## Shape Shoulder
**Next row.** Cast off 5[6:7:7:8]
sts in patt, patt to end.
11[12:14:15:17] sts.
**Next row.** Patt.
**Next row.** Cast off 5[6:7:7:8] sts
in patt, patt to end. 6[6:7:8:9]
sts.

**Next row.** Patt.
Cast off rem 6[6:7:8:9] sts in
patt.

## SLEEVES (Both alike)
Using 3¼ mm needles and
thumb method cast on
32[34:34:38:40] sts.
Work 4 rows in g-st as given for
Back.
Change to 4 mm needles and
work as follows:-
**1st row.** Knit.
**2nd row.** Purl.
These 2 rows are called **st-st**
(stocking stitch).
Work in st-st (throughout) inc 1
st at each end of 3rd and every
foll 4th[4th:4th:6th:6th] row to
38[38:44:54:52] sts.
Inc 1 st at each end of every

foll 6th[6th:6th:8th:8th] row to
44[48:54:58:62] sts.
Cont without shaping until
sleeve measures 16[19:23:28:32]
cm, 6¼[7½:9:11:12½] in, ending
with a ws row.
## Shape Sleeve Top
Cast off 4[3:3:3:3] sts at beg
of next 6[2:4:8:12] rows.
20[42:42:34:26] sts.
Cast off 5[4:4:4:4] sts at beg of
next 2[8:8:6:4] rows. 10 sts.
Cast off rem 10 sts.

## NECKBAND
Join shoulder seams.
With rs facing, using 3¼
mm needles, pick up and
knit 18[19:22:24:24] sts
evenly up right side of neck,
23[25:25:29:29] sts from back
of neck and 18[19:22:24:24] sts
evenly down left side of neck.
59[63:69:77:77] sts.
Work 4 rows in g-st as given for
Back.
Cast off knitways.

## LEFT FRONT BORDER
With rs facing, using 3¼ mm
needles, pick up and knit 3 sts
down neckband, 52[61:72:81:94]
sts evenly down front edge
and 3 sts down g-st border.
58[67:78:87:100] sts.
Work 4 rows in g-st as given for
Back.
Cast off knitways.

## RIGHT FRONT BORDER
With rs facing, using 3¼ mm
needles, pick up and knit 3 sts
up g-st border, 52[61:72:81:94]
sts evenly up front edge
and 3 sts up neckband.
58[67:78:87:100] sts.
Work 4 rows in g-st as given
for Back.
Cast off knitways.

## TO MAKE UP
Fold sleeves in half lengthways
and placing folds to shoulder
seams sew sleeves in position
12[13:14:15:16]cm, 4¾[5¼:5½:

6:6¼]in, from shoulder seams.
Join side and sleeve seams.
Sew 1 button just below neck
edge and 1 button level with
top of g-st ridge patt. Work 2
button loops to correspond. Pin
out cardie to the measurement
given. Cover with clean, damp
tea towels and leave until dry.
See ball band for washing and
further care instructions.

## Little Holiday Jacket
### BACK
Work as given for Back of Little
Holiday Cardie.

### LEFT FRONT
Work as given for Left Front of
Little Holiday Cardie to **.
Work 20[22:28:32:38] rows in
g-st ridge patt as given for Back.
**Shape Neck**
Work 6[8:6:7:5] rows dec
1 st at neck edge (end) of
next and every foll alt row.
22[24:28:29:33] sts.
Work 2[2:2:1:1] rows inc
1[1:1:2:2] sts evenly across last
row. 23[25:29:31:35] sts.
**1st row.** Knit to last 2 sts, k2tog.
22[24:28:30:34] sts.
**2nd row.** K1[0:1:0:1], * p3, k1,
rep from * to last 1[0:3:2:1] sts,
p1[0:3:2:1].
These 2 rows form **rib patt and
neck shaping**.
Work 23[23:27:31:35] rows
dec 1 st at neck edge in
3rd and every foll 4th row.
16[18:21:22:25] sts.
Cont in rib patt until left front
measures 28[32:38:42:48] cm,
11[12½:15:16½:19] in, ending
with a ws row.
**Shape Shoulder**
**Next row.** Cast off 5[6:7:7:8]
sts in patt, patt to end.
11[12:14:15:17] sts.
**Next row.** Patt.
**Next row.** Cast off 5[6:7:7:8] sts
in patt, patt to end. 6[6:7:8:9]
sts.
**Next row.** Patt.

Cast off rem 6[6:7:8:9] sts in
patt.

### RIGHT FRONT
Work as given for Right Front of
Little Holiday Cardie to **.
Work 20[22:28:32:38] rows in
g-st ridge patt as given for Back.
**Shape Neck**
Work 6[8:6:7:5] rows dec
1 st at neck edge (beg) of
next and every foll alt row.
22[24:28:29:33] sts.
Work 2[2:2:1:1] rows inc
1[1:1:2:2] sts evenly across last
row. 23[25:29:31:35] sts.
**1st row.** K2tog, knit to end.
22[24:28:30:34] sts.
**2nd row.** P1[0:0:2:1],
k1[1:0:1:1], * p3, k1, rep from *
to last 0[3:0:3:0] sts, p0[3:0:3:0].
These 2 rows form **rib patt and
neck shaping**.
Work 23[23:27:31:35] rows
dec 1 st at neck edge in
3rd and every foll 4th row.
16[18:21:22:25] sts.
Cont in rib patt until Right Front
measures 28[32:38:42:48] cm,
11[12½:15:16½:19] in, ending
with a rs row.
**Shape Shoulder**
**Next row.** Cast off 5[6:7:7:8]
sts in patt, patt to end.
11[12:14:15:17] sts.
**Next row.** Patt.
**Next row.** Cast off 5[6:7:7:8] sts
in patt, patt to end. 6[6:7:8:9]
sts.
**Next row.** Patt.
Cast off rem 6[6:7:8:9] sts in
patt.

### SLEEVES (Both alike)
Work as given for Sleeves of
Little Holiday Cardie.

### LEFT FRONT BORDER
With rs facing, using 3¼ mm
needles, beg at centre of
back neck, pick up and knit
11[12:12:14:14] sts from
back of neck, 26[28:30:33:35]
evenly down left side of neck,
32[38:50:56:67] sts evenly down

straight edge and 3 sts down
g-st border. 72[81:95:106:119]
sts.
Work 4 rows in g-st as given for
Back.
Cast off knitways.

### RIGHT FRONT BORDER
With rs facing, using 3¼ mm
needles, pick up and knit 3 sts
up g-st border, 32[38:50:56:67]
sts evenly up straight edge,
26[28:30:33:35] sts evenly
up right side of neck and
11[12:12:14:14] sts from back of
neck, ending at at centre of back
neck. 72[81:95:106:119] sts.
Work 4 rows in g-st as given for
Back.
Cast off knitways.

### TO MAKE UP
Fold sleeves in half lengthways
and placing folds to shoulder
seams sew sleeves in position
12[13:14:15:16]cm, 4¾[5¼:5½:
6:6¼]in, from shoulder seams.
Join side and sleeve seams.
Mark positions for buttons on
the Left Front for a girl and on
the Right Front for a boy. Sew 1
button just below neck shaping,
1 button 4 cm, 1½ in up from
lower edge and 1 button in
between. Work 3 button loops
to correspond. Pin out jacket to
the measurement given. Cover
with clean, damp tea towels and
leave until dry. See ball band
for washing and further care
instructions.

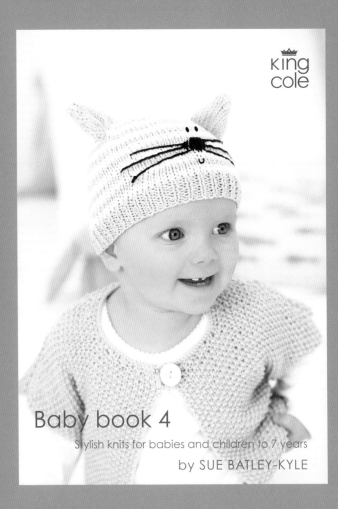

## Baby book 4

Stylish knits for babies and children to 7 years

by SUE BATLEY-KYLE

## Aran Book 2

34 Stylish knits from birth to 7 years

by SUE BATLEY-KYLE

# Other books by Sue Batley-Kyle

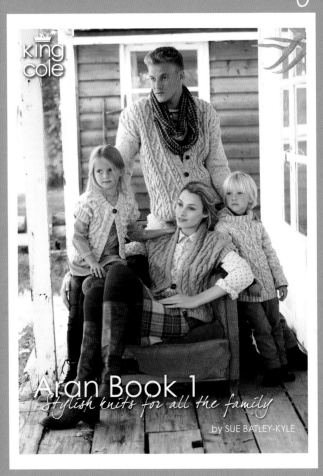

## Aran Book 1

Stylish knits for all the family

by SUE BATLEY-KYLE

## Baby book 5

35 Stylish knits for tiny premature to 18 month old babies

by SUE BATLEY-KYLE

## TENSION

**Very important**

It is essential to work to the stated tension to ensure success and you should always knit a tension square before starting the actual garment.

If you have too many stitches to 10cm, 4in, your tension is tight and you should change to a larger needle. If there are too few stitches, your tension is loose and you should change to a smaller needle.

Instructions are given for the smallest size, with larger sizes in square brackets. Where only one figure is provided, this applies to all sizes. Work all directions inside square brackets the number of times stated.

## WASHING INSTRUCTIONS

For optimum results it is always best to hand wash your King Cole garment.

**Baby Alpaca –** Hand wash only, dry flat, cool iron, do not tumble dry or bleach, can be dry cleaned.

**Bamboo Cotton DK –** Machine washable on a cool cycle, cool iron, do not tumble dry or bleach, can be dry cleaned.

**Cottonsoft DK –** Machine washable on a cool cycle, cool iron, do not tumble dry or bleach, can be dry cleaned.

**Merino DK –** Machine washable on a cool cycle, dry flat, cool iron, do not tumble dry or bleach, can be dry cleaned.

Also see individual ball bands for care instructions.

## GENERAL INFORMATION

The knitwear designs in this book are copyrighted and must not be knitted for resale. Reproduction of this publication is protected by copyright and is sold on the condition that is used for non commercial purposes.

Please note that all quantities in this book are based on average usage and therefore are approximate. We cannot accept responsibility for the finished garment if any other yarn than the one specified is used.

Owning to photography and printing restrictions the colour reproduction is matched as closely as possible to the yarn.

Although every effort has been made to ensure that instructions are correct the designer cannot accept any liabilities.

Printed by Fretwell Print & Design, Keighley, West Yorkshire

## ACKNOWLEDGEMENTS

BIG THANKS  - as always

To my amazing band of knitters, sewers, checkers and pattern writers, whose talents know no bounds – Adele, Alice, Angela, Carol, Carole, Delaine, Doreen, Irene, Jill,  Julie, Kath, Mary G , Mary W, Pauline, Sandra, Sarah,  Sue L, Sue W, Sue W ,Susan, Val and Wendi.

To the beautiful models for looking so adorable in their knits.

To Liz who always manages to create the most stunning shots and Claire who fashions the most gorgeous outfits to complement the knits, along with her talent for charming the little ones.

To Don, for his fabulous artwork, and attention to detail.

To Fretwell Printers, for their great service and whose quality of print, allows the images to shine.

To Rich and Tris for being with me every step of the way.

And Special thanks as always to Mike W for allowing me the opportunity to make my ideas a reality in this book.

THE QUEEN'S AWARDS
FOR ENTERPRISE:
2012

Merrie Mills, Snaygill Industrial Estate, Keighley Road, Skipton, BD23 2QR

Tel: 01756 703670 Fax: 01756 703680
Email: sales@kingcole.com    www.kingcole.com